CHANGE ELECTIONS TO CHANGE AMERICA:

DEMOCRACY MATTERS

Student Organizers in Action

CHANGE ELECTIONS TO CHANGE AMERICA:
DEMOCRACY MATTERS

Student Organizers in Action

JAY R. MANDLE
JOAN D. MANDLE

Foreword by Adonal Foyle

PROSPECTA PRESS

Prospecta Press
P.O. Box 3131
Westport, CT 06880
www.prospectapress.com

Paperback ISBN 978-1-935212-01-0
eBook ISBN 978-1-935212-02-7

Book and cover design by Barbara Aronica-Buck

CONTENTS

FOREWORD

Founding Democracy Matters was one of the most exciting and fulfilling things I have ever done. Working with students challenging the right of wealthy elites to use money to control the American political system has been exhilarating, an experience I never could have imagined growing up in Canouan, a tiny island in the Caribbean.

Even in those early years I was aware of politics. I was really, really angry at things I thought were unfair—that my family was so poor I sometimes didn't have enough to eat, that I was beaten by my teachers and picked on by other kids because I was so tall for my age. The calypso and reggae music that surrounded us brought powerful messages of oppression and empowerment.

But more significant for me as a young child was my personal experience with elections. For the 1,200 people living on Canouan, election days were major events. Each year, I watched as my uncle, the owner of a small grocery store, gave free drinks to anyone who said they would vote for his candidate. He then piled voters into his truck and took them to the polls. Uncle was a big man in Canouan because he could deliver votes. I didn't really understand what was happening, but I knew it was important, and that something about it was not right.

When, as a teenager, my adoptive parents, Joan and Jay Mandle, brought me to the United States, I became immersed in politics—but of a different kind. Joan and Jay were veterans of the civil rights movement, and as university professors were both deeply involved in researching and teaching about political and social change. I remember countless dinner conversations with their friends, all of whom argued passionately for hours about every issue under the sun.

At Colgate University I was a varsity basketball player and didn't have much time to do anything but study and play ball. But many of my friends were involved in volunteer work—at soup kitchens, with rape hotlines, creating a community garden, and serving as big brothers or sisters for at-risk local children. A turning point for me occurred one day in my favorite class, on philosophy and religion, during our in-depth study of student activism in the civil rights movement. Our professor accused us and our generation of being apathetic. I fought back, citing the volunteer activities of my friends and other students. I argued that we weren't apathetic at all, we cared about the world.

I never forgot that argument—especially since it went on for almost an hour after class ended and caused me to miss a basketball practice right before my team played a Patriot League Championship game. (We won anyway!)

Two years later, when I found myself playing in the rarified atmosphere of the NBA, I kept thinking back to that class. I realized that my professor was more right than I had given him credit for. I hadn't understood that he was talking about politics. He was saying that we in the 1990s, unlike the young people in the 1960s, lacked a significant political voice. On important public policy questions, ranging from health care and global warming to funding for higher education, students were silent. Because we did not engage in politics, we were not part of the country's decision-making process. "Apathetic" might not have been exactly the best word to describe us, but he certainly was correct that we possessed almost no influence on the critical political issues of the day.

The more I thought about young people's disengagement from politics, the more frustrated I became. I decided to try to use my celebrity status and my income as an NBA player to help overcome their political alienation. My work with Democracy Matters over the last thirteen years has proven just how rewarding—and how difficult—that task is.

Being part of Democracy Matters provided a focus of interest outside the pressures of my professional athletic career. Participating with DM students in their programs, projects, conferences, and meetings was both incredibly gratifying, as well as fun. The students' optimism, creativity, and enthusiasm inspired me. But Democracy Matters also gave me the opportunity to grapple intellectually with two important questions: first how to lessen the one-sided political power of the big campaign donors who are corroding our democracy; and second how to increase the political engagement of young people.

Over the years I have lectured on and discussed these issues at conferences, universities, law schools, and even more frequently, through the media. As an NBA player, I was already accustomed to interviews with sports reporters and radio and television commentators who focused on basketball, but soon they were questioning me often at length about Democracy Matters. I sensed that the juxtaposition of my love of basketball and my passion for political equality seemed odd to them.

But to me the connection was perfectly obvious. You only make it to the NBA on merit. No one gets there just because he is wealthy or can depend on someone who is. My teammates had no advantages but their talent. And on the court, a clear set of rules was (usually) administered fairly. Everyone was equal—no team is given extra points or any unfair advantage on the court. On a given night any team can win, depending only on how well they play. Basketball is a realm of fairness and justice. As a result, people love sports, admire athletes, and are horrified when cheating is exposed.

There is a perfect analogy in politics. If politics were just and fair, the people who make our laws would be chosen on the basis of merit, not money. Elections would be on a level playing field, not auctions that go to the highest bidder. And the rules of the game would fairly apply to everyone. Instead, unlike sports, politics and politicians are generally loathed, believed to work only for those who can "pay to play." My commitment to Democracy Matters stems from my desire for an inclusive democracy that is as fair and equal as sports competition.

This book captures Democracy Matters in all its dimensions— both successes and failures. It is an important record of young people's attempts, in the long tradition of grassroots student activism, to strengthen democracy and curb the political power of wealth. Young people in the past have helped to make this a more just and fair world. With organizations like Democracy Matters, I believe they can do it again.

Adonal Foyle, March 2014

PREFACE

Political and income inequality grow in tandem. The increased inequality in the first has its mirror image in the second. Because that is so, a self-reinforcing cycle is established. Those whose share of the national income grows are increasingly able to shape the political process to their own advantage. As a result, those of us who want to reverse the trend and achieve a more egalitarian America face a formidable challenge: how to reduce the political dominance of the super-rich at a time when those very individuals have been able to enhance their political clout.

There is only one way to counter the political power of wealth. Large numbers of people, mobilized in support of progressive legislation, are required. A social movement is needed. Such movements have secured big victories in the past and more recently. The ending of segregation and the securing of voting rights for black Americans was one such achievement. Another was the breaking down of gender barriers. A third has been the progress made by the lesbian, gay, bisexual, transgender and queer (LGBTQ) movement, especially with regard to the right to marry.

Yet with exception of the evanescent Occupy Wall Street effort, no movement to oppose the growth of political and economic oligarchy has appeared in the United States. That growth continues unimpeded.

We built Democracy Matters in the hope that it would help advance the creation of a progressive groundswell. Democracy Matters continues to organize students to promote the enhanced political equality that the public funding of election campaigns would secure. We wrote this book as a way to help others identify both the positive potential that exists in political organizing and the formidable barriers that make such an effort difficult. It is the story of Democracy Matters and its efforts to organize students to support campaign finance reform.

The political perspective and any mistakes in this book are our own. But we are deeply grateful to the following people who have encouraged and supported this book and our entire Democracy Matters journey: Jon Mandle, Adonal Foyle, Pat and Mike Burke, Daryn Cambridge, Amira Diamond, Bonnie Hallam, Anita Kinney, Megan Luce, Ben Shute, and Burt Weltman. Most of all we thank the thousands of students who through Democracy Matters have committed themselves to the hard work of fighting for a real democracy where people, not money, shape the world.

CHANGE ELECTIONS TO CHANGE AMERICA:
DEMOCRACY MATTERS
Student Organizers in Action

CHAPTER 1

MONEY AND POLITICS

Most people in the United States believe that the country's political system is broken. Congress is viewed with contempt. Polling data consistently reveal that the public believes elected officials respond primarily to special interests rather than to the needs and preferences of their constituents.[1] In this, popular attitudes are more right than wrong. Recent scholarship has concluded that in fact elected officials do grant more attention to their wealthy campaign contributors than to their middle-class and low-income constituents.[2]

Their doing so is the direct result of the fact that politicians depend on private donations to finance their election campaigns. Far fewer than one percent of the American population provides at least two-thirds of the campaign funds received by candidates for Congress and the Presidency.[3] By making those contributions, donors obtain influence that is denied to non-donors. Furthermore, contributor power was enhanced in 2010, first as a result of the Supreme Court's Citizens United decision and then by an Appeals Court judgment based on it (*SpeechNow.org v. FEC*). Those judgments established that no limits could be placed on the use of private, corporate, and union spending on political speech so long as those funds were not explicitly coordinated with the official campaigns of candidates. The result was a political campaign in 2011–12 like no other. Between 2008 and 2012 official campaign contributions grew by 30 percent, from $1.388 billion to $1.811 billion, while "outside expenditures"— unleashed by the courts—grew by almost tenfold from $147 million to $1.309 billion.[4] More than ever, the political system is awash in big private money.

The politicians who benefit most from these arrangements are those with their own wealth and/or networks of wealthy supporters. Candidates who lack such networks are likely to be badly outspent, placing them at a competitive disadvantage. But more than that, the need to be well financed from private sources bars most Americans from even contemplating the idea of standing for election. They simply cannot raise the money to be competitive. Thus it is that a small elite dominates the political process. A very limited segment of the population disproportionately influences who runs for office, who wins, and as a result the issues and policies that are legislated. In this way, private wealth has succeeded in undermining two basic democratic principles: every citizen should be able to run for office and everyone should possess equal influence in the political process.

It could be otherwise. The role of private wealth in politics would be significantly reduced if electoral campaigns were treated as public goods.[5] This is already the case in Maine, Arizona, and Connecticut, where candidates for state office can choose to finance their races with public funding. A similar system exists in cities including New York and Los Angeles where candidates can qualify for generous public funds to augment a limited ability to receive private contributions.[6]

Public subsidies through grants and/or matches of small private contributions allow candidates to compete with opponents who continue to rely only on private contributions. Because public financing is voluntary and private funding an option, it is constitutional; it does not violate First Amendment free speech rights. Would-be donors can still find outlets for their political contributions. But because of public funding, individuals without access to private wealth can nevertheless become viable candidates for office. In Maine, for example, between 2002 and 2010,the number of candidates for the state legislature grew from 98 to 111, an increase entirely due to the fact that the number of women running with public funding increased from 68 to 89.[7] These candidates, freed from attending fundraising parties and spending hours "dialing for dollars," can legitimately claim to be the candidates most accountable to voters.

The benefits of a public financing option extend beyond widening the range of policy alternatives and the candidates presented to the electorate. Just as important, public financing could help rebuild confidence in the American political system—and in democracy itself. With it, the laws and policies emerging from the political process would be more responsive to the preferences of voters than they are now. The legitimacy of the political system would increase as the impact of money and the power of wealth was reduced.

THE NEED FOR A SOCIAL MOVEMENT

Despite the widespread cynicism and anger generated by the flood of political money, a broad social movement demanding the public financing of election campaigns has not materialized. Such a movement is needed if sitting politicians are to be convinced to enact a public funding option for electoral contests. Today's politicians, donors, and corporate lobbyists at every level of politics are participants in and beneficiaries of a system that serves their interests. They are, after all, the people who have used it successfully. Incumbents and their patrons have a strong interest in maintaining the status quo. As a result, the best arguments for reform will continue to fall on deaf ears until and unless there is strong grassroots political pressure for change.

It will, however, not be easy to persuade the American people to exercise the necessary pressure on their representatives. Recognition of the political bias to wealth has led many to conclude that government will not ever be supportive of their interests. Instead of seeing the public sector as an ally and a source of support, as was the case overwhelmingly during the 1930s with the New Deal, many people today see the government as ineffective if not actually an enemy. Even though polling data suggest that large numbers believe there is a need to change how campaigns are financed, few actively seek government financing as the solution to the problem. Public campaign financing involves an increase in the role of government, and because of that it is dismissed as either unworkable or undesirable. That the government can be used to fix the problem of a biased government is a hard, but necessary, argument to make.

To most people, however, the conservative argument that government should be miniaturized is attractive only in the abstract. When it comes to specifics there is very little support for cutting the majority of government programs.[8] Thus, despite a seeming consensus to the contrary, Americans can be won over to support public expenditures. But their doing so requires that a convincing case be made that the middle class will be the beneficiaries. By the same token, as long as people are skeptical of such an outcome, they are likely to remain resistant to paying for electoral campaigns with their tax money. They will have to be convinced that a public funding option will result in reining in, to their benefit, the political power of wealth.

A great deal of persuasion needs to be done before the American people come to believe that the public funding of political campaigns would better serve them than the current system does. Advocates of public financing have to make a threefold argument. The first is that private campaign financing is the reason that the government today effectively serves neither the people nor the common good. The second argument is that public campaign financing is a necessary step to create a government that citizens can trust and that is accountable to them. As public financing erodes candidates' dependence on big donors, a more inclusive democracy and a truly representative government can be built. The third argument is that a system of publicly financing electoral campaigns has a reasonable chance of being adopted. What needs to be demonstrated is that ordinary citizens are capable of generating the power to compel reform, even in an initially unfavorable political environment. Cynicism has to be transformed into the hope that the power of numbers can trump that of wealth.

Achieving the public funding of election campaigns awaits the mobilization of a broad and powerful social movement demanding change. Such movements are vehicles not only for persuasion but also for the demonstration of power. Their demands illuminate the need for reform—what change would look like, and how such a change would benefit society. At the same time, by virtue of the numbers mobilized, social movements can exhibit political clout. They embody the leverage that can potentially move otherwise uninterested incumbent politicians to support reform—to force them to do what they otherwise do not want to do. And an active citizenry represents the votes that could enable pro-reform challengers to unseat resistant office holders and ascend to political office themselves. In the absence of such popular mobilization, reform advocates lack the tools to be either persuasive or politically credible. Without a social movement, the media—even when sympathetic to public campaign financing— will not provide the kind of sustained attention necessary to win over large numbers of people. Unless we can create local and regional grass-roots activism throughout the country, we will not be able to overcome the tag of political impotence.

HISTORY

Efforts to reform campaign financing in the United States date to the Progressive Era. In recent years these efforts have become intensified. Nevertheless they have not as yet been up to the task of putting a dent in the political power of wealth. Campaign finance reform has fallen short of democratizing politics in the United States.

In the aftermath of the 1960 election, concern over electoral finance surfaced among politicians. Television advertising had become increasingly important, and it was expensive. Many saw their careers threatened by the need to raise ever-larger amounts of campaign cash. By 1972, Democratic Party politicians were especially worried. In the presidential election that year, Richard Nixon's campaign raised and spent twice as much money as did his opponent, George McGovern.[9] It was this disadvantage, the historian Julian Zelizer writes, that "led more mainstream Democrats to support public financing and campaign regulations." These legislators in their turn joined ". . . experts, philanthropists, foundations and public interest groups" in a coalition that supported reforming the campaign financing system.[10]

Scandal provided the opening for this coalition to achieve at least a partial success. The break-in at the Democratic National Party Headquarters in the Watergate complex triggered investigations that revealed that Republican operatives had laundered political donations in order to disguise "dirty tricks" and illegal activities. With these revelations, the public interest in the role of money in politics grew and the reform coalition and its congressional allies seized the moment. In February 1972, Congress passed and President Nixon signed the Federal Election Campaign Act (FECA, later amended in 1974). The new legislation affected federal races and contained a variety of reforms: revenue reporting requirements; limits on political spending by candidates (almost immediately ruled unconstitutional by the Supreme Court in *Buckley v. Valeo*); limits on individual campaign contributions; and a system of public funding for presidential candidates.

FECA represented a substantial legislative accomplishment for the advocates of campaign finance reform. It significantly limited individual campaign contributions and for the first time enabled presidential candidates to run for office without depending exclusively on private donors. In exchange for agreeing to spending limits, candidates could receive public funding without strings attached.

FECA thus established the legitimacy of an alternative campaign funding mechanism.

Despite these achievements, the fact remains that FECA's impact fell far short of solving the problem of big private money in politics. The effort to include a provision for a public funding option for congressional races failed. Private donors continued to be the sole source of funding for Senate and House races. FECA did limit contribution levels to congressional candidates, though these far exceeded what most Americans could afford. Furthermore, the political clout of wealth was enhanced by the spread of a practice known as "bundling." This occurs when an individual "bundler" collects separate campaign contributions from family members, friends, colleagues, and other donors, and provides the pooled amount to a candidate in a lump sum. By calling on networks of other similarly situated people, wealthy individuals were able to retain their ability to turn the political donation spigot off or on and thus remain powerful political players.

The new presidential public financing system was also flawed. Though it included the option for presidential candidates to receive full public funding, it did so only for the general election. The law provided only matching funds for primary races. As a result, aggressive private fundraising early in the election cycle was imperative in order to secure the public matching funds necessary to run a competitive race. Since only wealthy donors, but not the general public, typically make large early investments in political races, big contributors continued to have a life and death choke-hold on the campaign viability of presidential candidates.

With the passage of time, a second flaw in the presidential funding system revealed itself. FECA mandated an inflation adjustment in presidential grants for each election cycle. This provision ensured that the purchasing power of public financing to presidential candidates would not decline. It failed to take into account, however, that the cost of campaigning would rise much more rapidly than the rate of inflation. The implication of this difference was made clear in the 2000 election. After FECA became law, every major presidential candidate opted to use the public financing system. But in 2000, for the first time, a major candidate, George W. Bush, chose to depend only on private fundraising for his ultimately successful primary race. By relying on private donations he was able to raise and spend more money than if he had been legally bound by the spending limits tied to the public financing option. By 2004 Democratic and Republican presidential candidates alike had forsworn public financing in primary elections. When in 2008 Barack Obama opted out of public financing in both the general election and the primary, and when in 2012 both major presidential candidates did so, the death knell was rung for FECA's presidential public financing system.

In 2002 the Bipartisan Campaign Finance Reform Act (BCRA) amended FECA with the ostensible purpose of regulating so-called "soft" money—donations to political parties and committees. The Act did accomplish that objective, but as with FECA, contained flaws that resulted in its doing little if anything to reduce the power of wealth in politics. Most striking was that BCRA doubled the so-called "hard" money limit—the amount of money an individual could legally contribute to a congressional candidate. As a result, during the 2011–12 electoral cycle, an individual was permitted to make $96,000 in campaign contributions: $2,500 to campaign committees for a primary election; $2,500 for a general election; $10,000 to political action committees (PACs); $60,000 to national party committees; and $20,000 to state and local party committees.[11]

Obviously, these increases were damaging to the cause of political equality. They were quickly dwarfed, however, by the flood of private, often undisclosed independent political expenditures triggered by both the January 2010 Supreme Court Citizens United decision and the March decision in the same year by the U.S. Court of Appeals for the District of Columbia in *SpeechNow.org v. the Federal Elections Committee*. In the first, the Court ruled that prohibiting corporations and unions from using their treasury funds for independent expenditures (those not explicitly linked to political campaigns) was unconstitutional. In the second, the Court of Appeals ruled that limits were not constitutionally permissible on contributions to political action committees (PACs) that undertook independent expenditures. In practice these decisions resulted in the formation of groups known as Super-PACs. When structured as charitable foundations or social welfare groups, these new entities not only were unrestricted in how much money they could raise and spend, but were not even required to divulge the names of their contributors. The upshot was a dramatic upsurge in this new form of political expenditures—by disguised political organizations, anonymously funded, spending unrestricted amounts of money. From negligible levels, this form of outside independent political expenditures increased to $454 million in 2010 and to $1.4 billion in 2012, $300 million of which came from undisclosed sources.[12]

Thus, even with the adoption of FECA and BCRA, private money continues to dictate the content of politics. In the first place, the high cost of running for office precludes most Americans from even considering the idea of doing so. They simply cannot raise the money. Secondly, candidates' financial dependency on private donors means successful politicians are not able to stray far from the policies and legislation their funders support. Doing so means risking a cut-off of funds and political oblivion. The consequence is that a small wealthy elite continues to dominate the funding of political campaigns.

That campaign finance reform has so far failed does not mean that reducing the role of private wealth in politics is an impossibility. Maine, Connecticut, Arizona, New York City, and other jurisdictions that have implemented public financing laws prove otherwise. Nor does it mean that the advocates of FECA and BCRA were incompetent. Lobbyists for Common Cause and other organizations were unstinting in their efforts to secure reform and accomplished a great deal by playing the inside-the-DC-Beltway game effectively. But that precisely was the problem. The politics of reform, to be transformative, require demands from the grassroots. Those demands have been lacking—a failure that was the inevitable result of the decision to pursue reform before attempting to build a broad reformist movement.

CHAPTER 2

GETTING STARTED

The Democracy Matters story begins during the late 1990s when we were temporarily living in Oakland, California. Disgusted by the extent to which private money was dominating the outcome of elections, we decided to see if, in the favorable atmosphere provided by the politically liberal Bay Area, we could launch the kind of grassroots movement for campaign finance reform that we thought the issue required.

We decided to do so at the municipal level. Our effort was aimed at getting the city of Oakland to adopt a system similar to the one employed in New York City. There, candidates for office receive a generous matching grant from the city in exchange for agreeing to limits on private contributions. This system had been in place for over a decade and had been remarkably successful. It effectively opened the electoral process to those who formerly had been shut out of the possibility of running for office. The method we chose was a tried-and-true approach: build a coalition of activists in support of the goal and with that in place hold meetings, house parties, and cultural events to convince as many people as possible that joining in the common effort was a good use of their time and energy.

But where to begin? Aware of the long-standing commitment to campaign finance reform of the national organization Common Cause, we contacted its California office. We found that California Common Cause was indeed interested in campaign finance reform as one of several "good government" issues, but it had neither local nor regional groups engaged in grassroots organizing. Its small staff, based in Sacramento, concentrated on building relationships with state legislators to press for the adoption of (or rejection) of specific legislation. Although California Common Cause had a skeletal plan for membership recruitment and citizen activism, it lacked both the personnel and the resources to implement its plan. There had been virtually no effort to develop local chapters, even in the Bay Area. Activists or potential activists were not being mobilized to work on any of Common Cause's priority issues, let alone campaign finance reform.

What the state organization did have, however, was a lengthy mailing list, contact information for hundreds of its members in the Bay Area. After considerable discussion and several trips to Sacramento, the director of California Common Cause agreed to allow us to try our grassroots organizing ideas. Armed with the membership list, we set out to build a Common Cause chapter of activists as a foundation upon to which to construct a movement to win public campaign financing in Oakland.

We did not trust email as the primary vehicle by which to build a chapter. Email is too often ignored and in any case is not sufficiently personal to be convincing. Instead, what it would take was a phone call and a serious conversation. And so it was that we spent the better part of two months calling through the list, often during the evening when people were likely to be home. It was in some ways a draining experience—phoning took a great deal of time and in the process we encountered some annoyed rebuffs. But we also tapped into a good deal of pent-up activism—people eager to use their energy politically but who had not found a way to do so. These were the people we were seeking. Our task was to engage them as participants in a cause whose objectives they agreed with, using tactics with which they were comfortable. Our basic point in these discussions was that a wide array of organizations and interest groups as well as individuals could benefit from an Oakland City Council with members not tied to private donors. Based on that assumption, the coalition we were attempting to construct would be diverse in both its thinking and composition. One issue would unite participants: the financing of election campaigns should be made more democratic.

Two months later we had a list of people who said they were interested in working on the issue and were willing to come to a meeting to discuss the creation of a Common Cause chapter whose focus would be the building of a reform coalition.

Close to forty people showed up at the first meeting, of those, a half-dozen later became core members of the chapter. We agreed to meet weekly at each other's homes, exploring the range of contacts we possessed, and thrashing out the issue of how the New York City system could be applied to much smaller and poorer Oakland. We fashioned our case for reform in light of the specific interests of the participating groups. Our group was well networked. Contacts were not a problem. Very soon we were in touch with all of the progressive groups in the city.

Our chapter developed a three-part plan: we would do the research necessary to develop a report that made the case for public financing in Oakland; we would build and sustain a coalition of local advocacy organizations and individuals to support a public financing bill; and we would meet with Council members to identify a legislator who would introduce and champion such a bill, and lobby other members for their support.

The members tasked with research sought advice from activists who had won full public campaign financing in Maine and Arizona. They also talked with members of the New York Campaign Finance Board who administered New York City's successful public financing system, and consulted with the staff at Public Campaign, a national organization that promoted public campaign financing. Common Cause's Oakland members examined the city's budget, and pored over the Oakland election reports that revealed how much campaign money candidates had raised and spent in the past. The document they produced outlined in detail the costs and benefits for Oakland of creating a public financing option for city races. It also provided specific language for a public financing bill. Later city lawyers would translate that into "legalese." The bill was ultimately introduced as the "Limited Public Financing of Elections Act of the City of Oakland."

In attempting to build a broad-based coalition, Common Cause Oakland reached out to over a hundred local organizations, sending them information on what we were doing, requesting invitations to speak at their meetings, and inviting them to join our coalition. The alliance that ultimately emerged was diverse in age, education, ethnicity, and the issues addressed. The core of the coalition—organizations whose members wrote letters, made calls, testified at hearings, and showed up at rallies—was principally made up of the Oakland League of Women Voters, Oakland ACORN, and student activists at the University of California, Berkeley, in addition to us in Oakland Common Cause. Other groups signed on in support of the legislation, though their members were less active than the core group. These included the Sierra Club, Oakland Democratic Party clubs, numerous neighborhood associations, and the local affiliate of the American Civil Liberties Union. A number of other organizations including religious groups and civic organizations like Rotary Clubs, though declining to publicly endorse our bill, contacted our Speakers Bureau to invite a representative to address their meetings. We were often able to recruit individual activists from those speaking opportunities.

At the end of a year of organizing an effective local coalition had emerged. Having created a strong foundation of grassroots support, we launched our campaign. Coalition members wrote articles in the local newspapers, did radio interviews, filled Speakers Bureau invitations, and provided testimony at City Council meetings. Rallies organized by the coalition were truly memorable, with their inspiring mix of age, ethnicity, class, and gender. And on December 14, 1999, after almost two years of local activism, the coalition won the day. Oakland's City Council passed a public financing option for candidates. Grassroots organizing had achieved a legislative triumph.

WORKING WITH STUDENTS

The victory in Oakland was grist for our organizing mill. After three years in the Bay Area, we knew we would soon be returning to our permanent home on the East Coast. We would bring with us a significant political triumph. The Oakland experience had given us reason to believe that it was possible to organize around the role of private money in politics. We knew that Oakland's hothouse environment of left politics was not representative of the political life we would find elsewhere. But we had learned that people could be mobilized in support of campaign finance reform and that our method of labor-intensive grassroots organizing worked. The question that arose for us as we traveled home was how we would build on our achievements in the Bay Area.

As college professors, it was perhaps unavoidable that our thoughts turned to students in thinking about what to do next. As a general principle, we believed that students would have to play a special role in a movement to reform campaign financing. Historically, young people have often provided a moral compass for their elders, highlighting the need for social change. They have also been an important source of energy and innovative thinking. As a result, the question we had to answer was whether a student movement could emerge as part of the broad effort at democratic renewal that we were envisioning.

Certainly there were grounds for skepticism. It has been half a century since America's campuses were the site of pitched political insurgencies in support of civil rights and in opposition to the war in Vietnam. Further, there is some evidence that today's contemporary young people have little interest in replicating the 1960s. Researchers at the University of California at Los Angeles who conduct annual national surveys of student attitudes, reported in 2011 that only 6 percent of first-year students thought there was a "very good chance" that they would participate in student protests or demonstrations. Among these students, the goal in life that scored highest as "essential" or "very important" was that of "being well off financially." Compared to the 79.6 percent of respondents who considered affluence a top priority, only 19.8 percent accorded "influencing the political structure" priority attention. Indeed, only 32.8 percent even believed that "keeping up to date with political affairs" was essential or very important. With these attitudes, it is no surprise to learn that the political self-characterization "middle of the road" was chosen by more students than any other classification (47.4 percent). Only 2.7 percent thought of themselves as "far left," with another 27.6 percent describing themselves as "liberal."[13]

When it came to students' responses to specific issues, however, the impression of bland disinterest looked considerably different. When the survey asked students their opinions on important political issues, their responses suggest that, notwithstanding the political labels they attach to themselves, the majority of students clearly fall on the progressive side of the political spectrum. The table below indicates that a majority—frequently a large majority—of college freshmen in 2011 were not only socially liberal with regard to issues of race, immigration, and gender, but they also did not want military spending increased. Large numbers agreed that the government should address climate change, ensure that everyone has access to adequate health care, and accord same-sex couples the right to marry. A similar conclusion concerning their progressive attitudes can be drawn by examining responses to two questions from an earlier UCLA survey. In that 2010 survey, 64.0 percent of respondents agreed that "wealthy people should pay a larger share of the taxes than they do now" and 67.5 percent believed that "the government should do more to control the sale of guns."[14] The progressive views possessed by students provide a foundation upon which a political movement might take root.

Beyond the views reported in surveys, the outpouring of involvement in Barack Obama's 2008 and 2012 campaigns by young people as well as their involvement in the Occupy Wall Street actions evidenced on many campuses in 2011 indicate that many students can be drawn into political activism under the right circumstances. But it is also the case that young people on campuses today share in the political cynicism that pervades the society. As a result, the burden falls on political organizers to demonstrate that the route to progress on all the issues

STUDENT POLITICAL ATTITUDES, 2011 (%)

Abortions should be legal.	60.7
Marijuana should be legalized.	49.1
Racial discrimination is no longer a major problem in America.	24.5
Same-sex couples should have the right to legal marital status.	71.3
Federal military spending should be increased.	30.5
Undocumented immigrants should be denied access to public education.	43.0
A national health plan is needed to cover everybody's medical costs.	60.5
Addressing global warming should be a federal priority.	63.2

Source: John H. Pryor, Linda DeAngelo, Laura Palucki Blake, Sylvia Hurtado, and Serge Tran, *The American Freshman: National Norms Fall 2011* (Berkeley/Los Angeles/ London: University of California Press, 2011), 39.

that concern students is activism aimed at achieving a public financing option for candidates.

We thought that in the wake of our public financing success in Oakland, Common Cause at the national level might be open to taking on a new initiative—a grassroots organizing project with young people as its focus. Common Cause possessed the positive national reputation, the resources, and the professional staff that could make such a project work. Furthermore, it was widely known that the organization was plagued by a rapidly declining and aging membership. To recruit young people and train them as future activists might be an attractive new departure. But as it turned out, the Common Cause leadership was not interested in going in that direction. We were on our own.

Well, not entirely. Our adopted son, Adonal Foyle, had just signed a lucrative contract as a player in the National Basketball Association. With the contract in hand, our family discussions turned to how Adonal could use his privileged economic status to make a difference in the world. The bulk of his income would of course be invested safely, so as to ensure that when his career as an athlete came to an end (the average is about four years in the NBA), he would have a well-secured nest egg. But beyond this lay the question of how he would "give back," the cliché often used by athletes to describe their charitable contributions to local groups. From the beginning, Adonal made it clear to us that he did not want to follow that pattern. We explored many ideas, but when the question arose of whether the kind of organizing that had been successful in Oakland might serve as a model for creating activism among college students, Adonal seized on the idea. Excited by the idea of students working together to deepen democracy, he ultimately settled on campus organizing for public financing as the issue he wanted to support.

And so in the fall of 2000, Democracy Matters was born on the Colgate University campus. Settling on Colgate as a pilot for the project seemed obvious. As faculty members we knew and had access to large numbers of students there, and as a famous alumnus, Adonal was sure to attract attention as well. We also liked the fact that Colgate did not possess a culture of political activism. It would present us with a demanding test. We thought that if Democracy Matters resonated with a broad spectrum of Colgate students, we would be justified in believing that our project would work on other campuses as well. If not, we would have to reassess.

In deciding on the organization's structure we called on Joan's nine years of experience as the director of Women's Studies at Colgate. In that position, she had established a Center for Women's Studies. Each year, Joan selected a dozen work-study students to engage in campus organizing projects focused on issues of feminism and social change. The goal was to involve the entire campus—faculty, students, and administrators—in thinking and talking about these issues. Joan and her full-time program assistant trained and supported the students as they developed ways to engage others through film series, brown-bag lunch dialogues, and educational poster campaigns, as well as projects that reached beyond the campus such as participation at conferences, and discussions with high school students in local schools.

It was this experience that shaped our decisions concerning Democracy Matters' structure. We would offer a Democracy Matters internship to an undergraduate on each campus, a DM campus coordinator. He or she would be supported in their organizing by the

Democracy Matters field staff, each of whom would closely mentor and work with a number of campuses. The design was intended to create a core of dedicated and accountable interns, and at the same time provide them with the support necessary to build and lead strong campus chapters.

Very early on we made a decision to provide a financial stipend to our interns. On the one hand, we wanted to ensure that Democracy Matters had a diverse pool of applicants. Without providing a stipend, we were concerned that we might not be able to include students from low-income families. We did not want only wealthy students or elite schools to be part of Democracy Matters. In addition, offering to pay for political organizing would indicate the seriousness with which we were approaching the internship work. While we recognized that a stipend might attract some applicants who were more interested in a paycheck than in political organizing, our commitment to inclusivity weighed more heavily in the balance. Furthermore, we were confident that we could weed out students who were not fully committed to political organizing. It would quickly become obvious to students that taking on a Democracy Matters internship would be both difficult and demanding—not an undertaking for the faint of heart.

Even before we had finalized these and other organizational details, we decided to go ahead with the Colgate pilot program at the beginning of the fall semester. We recruited Mary, a Colgate senior political science major, as our first intern.[15] We chose her primarily on the basis of our knowing her to be smart and hardworking, and that she was intrigued by the issue and project when we discussed it with her. But the reality was that Mary possessed only the most super-ficial knowledge of the political role of private campaign funding in

American elections. She had literally never heard of publicly financed campaigns. As a result, before the semester began we engaged in an informal crash course with her, so that when students arrived on campus she would be able to get to work.

As it turned out, the fact that Mary had never been politically active nor conversant with our issue provided us with a better test of the viability of our model than we had anticipated. Over the years, the political views of many students who became campus coordinators were similar to Mary's. They sensed that private wealth was distorting the political process, but they were hazy about solutions for the problem and in addition were new to activism.

As early as November it had become clear that Democracy Matters at Colgate was flourishing. Mary worked hard, warming to her task, and attracted a core group of active members to the chapter. Mary and other "DMers" published articles in the school paper, gave "DM raps" in classes, and organized a petition-signing campaign in support of public financing which they later sent to state legislators. In addition, they taught several classes about money in politics at local high schools, and staged an on-campus "Democracy Rally" for public campaign financing. We started making plans to expand to more colleges and universities.

One serious problem did present itself. Our success raised the difficult question of who would manage an expanding Democracy Matters. Directing the organization as well as mentoring Mary and the other students had proven to be very time-consuming for us. We were able to handle running the pilot project along with our professorial responsibilities, but it was obvious that if we were to expand we would need a full-time director. The organization had to be administered;

staff and students had to be hired, funding raised, materials ordered, and paychecks issued on time. We also needed to cultivate the media, manage relationships with universities and other reform organizations, and recruit new campuses and students. Furthermore, our campus coordinators, well intentioned though they might be, would not be equipped to do their jobs effectively without intense training, guidance, and support throughout the year. An effective executive director of Democracy Matters would have to be a teacher, an organizer, and a fundraiser, in addition to being an administrator.

The obvious candidate for this position was Joan. The problem was that she would have to turn away from a twenty-five-year career of successful teaching and research as a professor of sociology. She would have to leave Colgate and give up the security of tenure for the uncertainty of the world of political organizing and nonprofit fundraising. The truth was that despite the success of our first year, we really had no idea whether or how long DM would last. But ultimately Joan bit the bullet: she resigned from her position at Colgate to lead Democracy Matters.

CAMPUS COORDINATORS

We had established that it was possible for a DM chapter to do good work. But we had not yet decided on the standards we would employ in selecting campus coordinators. Without giving it a great deal of thought we had envisioned filling these internships with student activists who shared three characteristics: 1) they would understand the class bias of the political system and how it overrepresents the rich and underrepresents everyone else; 2) they would understand themselves to be political radicals who saw the need to finance electoral campaigns publicly before a progressive political project could be viable; and 3) they would be independent of the Democratic Party, but would see the importance of engaging members of the Party in order to secure legislation. Related to these three was a fourth characteristic. To become a DM campus coordinator meant taking on a time-consuming, laborious, and often frustrating task. The idea of public financing of electoral campaigns was nowhere on the political agenda. Whatever the politics possessed by the campus coordinator, he or she would be taking on an arduous task.

Aside from a willingness to take on a difficult job, the students we successfully recruited to become campus coordinators almost never satisfied these criteria. With few exceptions, we did not recruit the radical students we thought we would attract. Our experience has been that many self-defined student radicals, believing that American society is irremediably corrupted and beyond salvation, reject activism that engages the electoral system. Electoral politics in particular is seen at best as irrelevant—typically not even part of the conversation—or at worst as itself a mechanism of oppression. Politicians are widely viewed as dishonest, out of touch, unprincipled, and uninterested in the needs of ordinary people. Involvement with such politics—including efforts to change it such as ours—is perceived as both futile and personally corrupting. From the perspective of these students, Democracy Matters looked naïve in its analysis and too tame in its goals—and therefore was doomed to failure.

Other activists shied away from Democracy Matters because they were not willing to move away from the single issue they were working on. The single largest grouping of activists on campuses in 2001 was concerned with environmental issues, including but not confined to the problem of global climate change. Much of this concern, however, was and still is devoted to local and localized issues. Students frequently addressed the environmental impact of the campus on which they resided, focusing, for example, on recycling. More society-wide issues such as cap-and-trade systems or carbon taxation were accorded little attention. The impact of energy company political donations on environmental policy was at best an after-thought.

Furthermore, students majoring in academic subjects to which socially conscious students typically gravitate –sociology, peace studies, or black or women's studies—only rarely applied for a DM internship. These are subject areas that tend to present a radical critique of American society. Though our internship was explicitly focused on political organizing for social change, few such students were interested. In explaining this anomaly, our speculation is that the academic majors that attract activist students actually give little emphasis in the curriculum to the feasibility of political and social change. Instead these disciplines examine what is wrong—the history of, sources of, and present forms of inequality, discrimination, or prejudice. Much less frequently are potential solutions to the problems explored. Indeed, what is often implicitly conveyed is that the problems are so overwhelming that social change is simply impossible.

A counterpart to our misjudgment concerning DM's attractiveness to radical students was our failure to anticipate that a majority of our intern applicants would be political science majors. This miscalculation had to do with the reputation of political science as a discipline that predominantly attracts politically moderate and conservative students. The typical political science undergraduate is thought to be more oriented to mainstream politics and/or law careers than to progressive social movements. We simply did not expect these students to be interested in an internship like ours, involving a deep critique of the political process and the advocacy of radical change.

But we were wrong. The political science majors attracted to Democracy Matters were typically those who were disappointed that our political system failed to live up to the truly representative and accountable ideal that they had studied. At the same time, they retained enough faith in the American system to believe that it could be reformed. Familiar with the structure of the political system, it was not a stretch for them to see how it might be used to correct its many problems and inequities. Many political science candidates for campus coordinator told us that they hoped Democracy Matters would help them to put into action the ideals of democracy they believed in. Others were motivated to become active because they were frustrated that their peers were so apathetic or hostile toward politics. We often heard about how frequently their friends rolled their eyes when politics was mentioned. In short, political science students who were interested in DM internships tended to take seriously the values of fairness, equal opportunity, and citizen responsibility that they had been taught were part of American politics. Many hoped that by working with Democracy Matters they could help restore those values.

Despite an interest in politics, most internship applicants lacked political organizing experience. Other than perhaps interning in the office of an elected official, most candidates lacked what they described as any "real" involvement with politics. Indeed, before applying to Democracy Matters many had never done anything more political than vote. But they had been part of organizations. Almost every applicant had been a member of one or more community service groups in high school or college, volunteering in hospices and soup kitchens, tutoring children, or raising money for breast cancer research or disaster relief. Some also reported participating in efforts to address campus-centered issues: aspects of student life such as the food service, dorm rules, incidents of date rape or racist speech.

However, among all our interns—formerly activist or not—only a very few had given much thought to campaign financing. Like most Americans, they were concerned that the huge amount of money going to candidates was corrupting and somehow unfair—but that was usually as far as it went. And almost no one knew that public financing was available to candidates in several states and cities throughout the country or that such a system was constitutional. They possessed remarkably little information about social movements, radical critiques of the political structure, or the history of efforts at social and political change in the United States or elsewhere.

We clearly had a great deal of teaching to do!

The small number of campus radicals who did apply for internships often turned out to be our best organizers. Though not involved in electoral politics, they brought experience from their activism on other issues, as well as wide-ranging contacts among students and campus organizations to DM. Furthermore, their insights into issues of money and politics were informed by their immersion in the organizing they had previously done on issues like tuition increases, sweatshops, inequality, or the environment. Radicals, more than most, saw that those problems were rooted in politics, and that the country's politics was biased. They often explained that even when they were actively involved trying to solve one problem, they were frustrated that they were neglecting other perhaps equally important issues. It was often their growing doubts about the efficacy of addressing a single social or economic problem in isolation that had led them to Democracy Matters.

In addition, these students understood well the difficulties associated with campus activism. A number of them reported that they were turning to Democracy Matters because of their disappointment with many of the campus groups in which they had participated. Over and over we heard complaints about student groups that were poorly organized and accomplished little, forming quickly and then soon falling apart. This seemed especially true for groups that emerged in response to specific current events—for instance, the war in Iraq or the BP oil spill in the Gulf of Mexico. These groups, applicants reported, had little staying power after a burst of activity as members shifted to other causes or simply gave up after only a few months or even weeks. Campus activists who became Democracy Matters interns were often seeking an organization that would be there for the long haul. They brought with them an understanding that making deep change requires hard work and a long-term commitment.

Finally, student activists were attracted to Democracy Matters because they wanted to join a movement that took political action. One applicant who became a DM intern at Vassar and later a Democracy Matters staff member, shared that goal. Arn had been deeply involved in LGBTQ organizing both in high school and during his first year in college. He had grown frustrated that the college LGBTQ group was primarily interested in holding meetings to discuss personal issues. He told us that he became increasingly convinced that political engagement was necessary in order to achieve LGBTQ's goals. The group resisted his argument that it should join with national activists promoting a civil rights agenda. Radical students like Arn—committed to an ambitious agenda of political change—found in Democracy Matters a home for the advocacy of practical political solutions.

CHAPTER 3

MENTORING

An organization like Democracy Matters succeeds or fails based on the skills of its campus coordinators. This reality confronted us with two key questions: How do we identify who might become effective organizers; and how do we train those people to reach their potential? Answering those questions put us and the students with whom we work on steep learning curves.

As we discussed earlier, most of the students who become campus coordinators for Democracy Matters know very little about political organizing when we first encounter them. They recognize the injustice that is present in a political system that provides disproportionate influence to wealthy campaign contributors. Further, they feel a personal responsibility to do something about that inequity. It is this sense of obligation that led to their decision to apply for a DM internship. But because they have only a superficial knowledge of past struggles for social justice, they possess little insight not only into the heroism of those efforts but their weaknesses as well.

In contrast, participants in the civil rights, antiwar, and feminist struggles had learned from activists in earlier movements. They mentored us even when their advice was not particularly welcomed. We profited not only from the positive lessons they imparted but as well from our own evaluations of where they had gone wrong. In the absence of such mentoring, most students who come to Democracy Matters have little concept of how difficult grassroots political organizing is or the frustrations that await them. But they are also unfamiliar with the exhilaration associated with hard-won movement triumphs.

As the political inexperience of the students who applied to DM became clear, we were forced to change our selection process. We scaled down our political expectations and instead sought students sympathetic to our cause, who possessed the personal characteristics that we hoped would allow them to become effective organizers. We tried to identify potential rather than assess experience.

We initially thought that applying for a Democracy Matters internship would only involve the submission of a resumé that included information about political involvement and organizing experience. That would allow us to make an initial cut to be followed by a phone or personal interview. However, when it became apparent that we did not have a large pool of applicants already schooled as political activists, we decided to require a cover letter to gain additional information. Candidates were asked to describe why they wanted to intern with Democracy Matters and what they hoped to accomplish politically. While this addition did yield useful information, it too failed to identify who might be the best organizers.

The interview thus became the heart of our selection process. Joan talked with each applicant, in conversations that often extended for more than an hour—in person whenever possible, or by phone or

Skype when necessary. She did not allow the interview to linger on the information provided by the students in their resumé or cover letter. She did not evaluate candidates on the basis of their knowledge of the role of money in politics or public financing issues. By then Joan knew we would have to teach most interns about these issues. Instead, what she tried to elicit was the extent to which the candidate possessed the intangibles that make an effective political organizer. She probed each person's willingness to defend unorthodox ideas, and assessed their patience and determination to work hard and continue in the face of setbacks. She explored with them what they most cared about and why, and asked about their families and friends. She asked them about how their studies related to their interest in Democracy Matters and what they thought about DM's potential for growth on their campus. The exhaustive nature of these discussions gave her insight into the probability that a student would succeed in what was sure to be a demanding internship.

In addition to encouraging the students to talk about themselves, Joan spent a considerable amount of time discussing Democracy Matters with them. Especially important was explaining why we had selected money and politics as our priority. To introduce the subject, she asked students to tell her about how the area that was most important to them—for example, the environment, the cost of higher education, civil rights—was affected by the system of campaign funding. Once their special concern was identified, the conversation explored how policy in that area was biased to reflect the interests of campaign donors and how public financing could end that bias. These interviews often concluded with students expressing amazement at how little they had known about money in politics.

Despite these efforts, and even after more than a decade of experience, we have never been able accurately to predict who would be successful as a campus coordinator. We usually had enough information to eliminate some candidates. There were almost always applicants who revealed—often inadvertently—that they had applied largely because of the stipend attached to our internship. Some prospective interns were so highly partisan, so strongly identified with a political party or candidates (almost always Democrats) that we worried about their effectiveness in an organization that would be as critical of that party as it was of the Republican Party. Students who wanted to focus only on non-controversial issues such as voter registration were also rejected.

Yet there were always a considerable number of applicants remaining with whom we were eager to work. Though perhaps lacking in detailed knowledge, these students possessed sensitivity to the inequality built into the current system and were eager to seek a means to change it. Both attributes were important. They had to understand the issues involved but also see themselves as political activists and change agents. Particularly important was an ability to be self-starters. In most cases Democracy Matters clubs had to be constructed from scratch. At least in the beginning the campus coordinators would be on their own.

Another important goal was to nurture DM's continuity on a campus. Because starting up is difficult, we particularly valued students who were reapplying for the campus coordinator position after having filled that role during the previous academic year. The longer a chapter remained active, the stronger it grew. If the campus coordinator was not returning, the next best candidate for the position was often someone who had been an active member of that DM chapter. Sometimes the chapter itself would hold an election and recommend a person for the position. Though we interviewed every applicant, we almost always concurred with the students' choice.

In selecting interns, we wanted to ensure that Democracy Matters included different ethnic, religious, class, and geographic backgrounds. We were particularly eager to enlist first-generation college students. We also thought it was important to have chapters at different kinds of colleges and universities. In practice this often involved giving special attention to candidates attending community colleges and historically black campuses and students from the South and the Southwest.

By July, having selected a pool of interns too large for Joan alone to mentor, we recruited a field organizer as a second DM staff member. At the same time, we asked each campus coordinator to begin to prepare for the internship. They were to study four online training modules on money in politics and four on campus organizing. We encouraged them to email us questions and/or comments concerning what they had read. In August, if we had enough interns in a particular region we conducted a day-long training session. We held similar training sessions by phone with other interns. We wanted to be confident that when school started, all our interns understood and were comfortable talking about the role of private money in politics and about successful public financing systems.

With the start of the academic year, our mentoring intensified. Intern and staff interaction was regularized. Weekly phone calls included discussions intended to reinforce what had already been covered in our initial training sessions, and to bring the students up to date on recent political developments that involved the role of money in politics. We sent a monthly *Democracy Matters E-News* to interns and all chapter members. This online newsletter was also sent to faculty, administrators, and other Democracy Matters friends and supporters. It featured wide-ranging discussions on money in politics, "factoids," and a "Money on My Mind" column in which Jay looked at how campaign funding related to current events. The *E-News* also reported on articles published by DM students in school newspapers, as well as those appearing in the national press written by DM staff and board members, like Jay's article in the *Washington Post*, "The Small Donor Fallacy." All of this, as well as Joan's bi-weekly emails with organizing ideas for campus coordinators provided DMers with an ever-deepening stock of information.

We wanted internships to provide students with a valuable learning experience. We did not want to force them, with little feedback or follow-up, to try to master the details of a complicated issue that was new to them. Our emphasis on continuous learning sets Democracy Matters apart from most other student organizations. In contrast to DM, they typically organize "boot camps" that bring students together for only one day or at most a weekend training session. These brief encounters impart useful and important information about organizing and politics, but we as teachers know that they are trying to do too much in too little time. One such national organizational training session we attended even included a two-hour "speed dating" organizational fair. In it, students were given less than five minutes to talk with a representative of each of more than thirty different non-profit organizations. After four minutes, a bell signaled that it was time to move on to talk with the next organization's representative.

This is simply bad pedagogy. Inundating young people with information crammed into two days is not how effective learning takes place. No doubt such exposure is better than nothing, but it is far better to provide time for reflection and staff/student interaction and follow-up. The fact that our learning process extended over an entire academic year gave DM interns the opportunity to develop their own ideas about the relationship between political power and the use of wealth, as well as what to do about it.

TEACHING ORGANIZING

Although a considerable part of our training centered on exploring issues of money and politics, we also needed to teach our interns about grassroots organizing. We did not want them to be only well-informed policy wonks. We needed to teach them to be effective organizers who could apply their knowledge to building a movement for change. Engaging in effective political activism was a different matter altogether from mastering the academic side of this project.

For virtually all our interns, learning how to become effective organizers was much harder than understanding how wealth exercised influence in the political process. What compounded the problem was that DM campus coordinators had to function as organizers right from the start, at the beginning of the academic year. They had to learn to quickly recruit other students to work with them as core members of their fledgling clubs. To do so they needed to compete with a plethora of other campus organizations trying to attract students. Without the luxury of time to build up organizing experience, our interns had to out-organize other groups and convince students that Democracy Matters was worth joining. And of course Democracy Matters was always at a distinct disadvantage in this competition compared to non-political groups. The alienation from and cynicism toward politics on campuses constituted a huge barrier.

Our online training modules, intensive in-depth conversations with our field staff, weekly phone calls, and campus visits did expose interns to the basics of organizing. But because our campuses were as varied as the skills and interests of our interns, each situation was unique. The demands of good organizing at a large university with many thousands of students, for example, are not the same as those at a small liberal arts college. Religiously affiliated colleges present a different organizing challenge than do public secular institutions. Organizing techniques that could bring success at geographically isolated campuses often are likely to be ineffective at urban schools. We worked closely with our students, to help them understand and react to the specific situation on each campus, crafting organizing strategies that fit very different circumstances.

It was sometimes difficult to convince our interns that no manual could fully explain how to be a successful organizer. There are of course general organizing guidelines. We taught campus coordinators the importance of mapping their campuses to identify the resources available and the groups that were most likely to be open to cooperating with Democracy Matters. We encouraged them to delegate tasks so that members would take ownership of the chapter. It was also important for our interns to build personal relationships and group solidarity in order to retain active members. DM meetings had to be interesting and fun. We explained that effective organizing requires creating multiple ways of repeating and disseminating the basic message—flyers, discussions, improvised skits and class presentations. We helped each campus coordinator to develop his or her own strategy, set of techniques, and implementation plan. But they also had to learn by doing.

This process was far from smooth; recurring problems surfaced each year. There were always some interns who were stymied by their worry that they needed to learn still more about money and politics before they could begin to organize. Even with our staff's assurance that they had a more than adequate understanding of the issue, these campus coordinators continued to agonize about what they perceived as their insufficient knowledge. Political science majors were often the worst offenders in this regard. Some of them seemed to have an almost infinite number of questions about the intricacies of campaign financing reform. They were concerned that someone might request information or make an argument they were unprepared to answer. It was never entirely clear to us whether such students were simply perfectionists—needing to feel they knew everything—or whether their hesitation concealed a fear of trying to organize. Or perhaps both.

Working with such students, we explained that it was simply not possible for anyone to fully master a subject that, like campaign financing, was changing all the time. It was equally impossible to be prepared to answer every imaginable question. We advised that if they were stumped by a query they should promise to check on it and get back to the questioner. Our staff would reassure interns that they could turn to them for help at any time. We also emphasized to the coordinators that they were much more likely to have success by emphasizing equality, fairness, and democracy than by detailing the complicated nuances of campaign financing legislation. The specifics could come later, but it was the deep egalitarian values advanced by public financing of elections that would be most effective in raising awareness of the need for reform and moving people to action. We insisted that students had to get on with the real goal of their internships — campus political organizing.

After a few weeks, most students overcame their need for perfection and/or their fear—at least enough to begin to organize. But there were always a few who persisted in begging for just a little more time to study the issue and master more policy details. One coordinator, from Georgetown University in Washington, DC, even insisted that she needed to write her own public financing bill. For these students, a Democracy Matters organizing internship was not a good fit and sometimes we had to withdraw their internship.

Another issue that troubled many interns was the question of how to effectively lead an organization. Perhaps because they were Democracy Matters interns—with an emphasis on the word *democracy*—some were reluctant to exercise leadership. In the most extreme cases they suffered from the view that their preparing an agenda for meetings, suggesting ideas or making decisions, might be somehow undemocratic. They did not understand that active leadership is compatible with democracy. In the absence of leadership, meetings would become disorganized, plans left undeveloped, and implementation weak. Members would drift away. We certainly did not want our campus coordinators to become autocrats. But we urged them to recognize that their job was to lead the DM chapter on their campus.

Some interns became frustrated because they were not able to elicit from other students a level of commitment comparable to their own. We explained that was an unreasonable expectation. But what they could and should do was encourage members to be actively involved—to voice their opinions, suggest their own ideas for chapter events, and take on chapter responsibilities. We wanted our interns to become mentors to other students. Although coordinators had primary responsibility for the chapter, we insisted that they create an environment that encouraged, respected, and developed others' abilities and talents.

One additional problem that plagued us every year was that many interns had inflated expectations about what they could accomplish. Excited about what they were learning concerning money, politics, and organizing, many initially believed that they could motivate large numbers of their peers to respond enthusiastically to Democracy Matters. They greatly underestimated how hard it would be to attract and retain chapter members. Many expected students and faculty to attend their events and participate in Democracy Matters programs in droves. In her 2004 end of semester report—a report that all interns submitted twice a year—Jen, a student at Reed College in Portland, Oregon, put it this way: "When I started out I couldn't believe that anyone would disagree with public financing of elections. It was such a great system that could solve so many problems, such a great opportunity to really do something. I thought it was a no-brainer. But it was really hard to get people involved."

This excessive optimism existed especially among students who had not done any previous political organizing. Their expectations about what would happen once they got started with DM was often based on their prior high school or college successes in organizing charity events, leading sororities or fraternities, or serving in student government. In his application for a DM internship, Matt, a junior at Marquette University in Milwaukee, described with well-deserved pride how he had organized a successful campus effort resulting in the donation of over 1,000 cans of food to a local food bank. Similarly, Seth at the University of California at Los Angeles wrote of his experience sponsoring an AIDS walk where hundreds of students raised money for stricken children. Such students felt sure that they could replicate their past successes with similar triumphs for Democracy Matters. Others, especially at the beginning of the academic year, declared that they would have no problem building a large DM chapter because so many students had already said they were interested in the organization. These interns believed that their own enthusiasm about political organizing could not help but be contagious—and that others would share their excitement.

Yet once DM interns began to try to organize on money and politics, reality brought them up short. Programs and events failed to attract the numbers they anticipated. Large rooms were left only partially filled. Despite their best efforts, they could recruit only a handful of committed chapter members. With these kinds of setbacks, many campus coordinators became discouraged. They began to doubt their ability ever to become successful organizers. They had not understood how different *political* organizing was from their earlier experiences. They did not anticipate the political disengagement they would face.

Some reacted by trying to hide their difficulties from the staff. Others, consciously or unconsciously, responded by retreating from organizing. As disappointments occurred, we worked with our interns to help them gain perspective. They needed to develop expectations that were more consistent with the difficulties of doing Democracy Matters–style politics. Our politics was unlikely to attract large numbers. DM's potential recruiting base was drastically more limited than, say, if an organizer initiated a march to raise money for AIDs research. There was an opposition to the reform we were proposing. Nevertheless, we assured them, success was possible if expectations were scaled down.

And success was important if DM chapters were to thrive. For that reason, our interns needed to learn how to use organizing techniques that would maximize DM's effectiveness and achieve the level of success realistically attainable. If an intern reserved a space for a large audience, for example, it would look depressingly empty when a smaller crowd showed up. The same number of attendees in a smaller room would feel like a victory. Or perhaps campus coordinators could have spread their message better with presentations in dorms or classes where they would have a captive audience, rather than by relying on posters to draw students to a forum or discussion. We taught our coordinators to distinguish mistakes caused by their inexperience from the inevitable setbacks that were beyond their control. Most important, as we emphasized over and over again, being a successful political organizer required patience and determination. It meant learning to cope with disappointment, not taking rebuffs personally, being willing to try new solutions, and most of all, not giving up.

An important point in all of this was to teach our coordinators that organizing success was often difficult to measure. Sometimes it felt that no progress was being made. But by staying with it, they were doing something important: working to open students' minds and offering them the opportunity to become politically engaged. We reminded them that deep social change is slow. There is no doubt that a reform as radical as reducing the political power of wealth would be a long time in coming. Historical perspective was important. The movements for women's suffrage and the civil rights of African Americans were struggles that took decades before they finally succeeded.

In sum, our mentoring offered our interns a perspective that could help them understand how important and difficult organizing is. We pointed out that by working with Democracy Matters, they were part of a long tradition of those who have fought the hard political fights for social justice and democracy. We taught them to understand that small victories are critical. Every time a DM student put up a newsletter or poster, handed out flyers, made a classroom presentation, or engaged another student in conversation, a success was achieved. DM activists might not be able to measure how many students they influenced. They would not know who would notice for the first time the harmful effects of private campaign funding, who might talk with their family or friends about public financing, decide to come to a meeting, or even someday work for reform. But as DM activists they were planting the seeds needed for the emergence of a social movement.

THE DM SUMMIT

Each year we organize a "Democracy Matters Summit" to bring together our coordinators and as many other DMers as possible. We want to create an environment in which they can interact, learn from one another, share experiences, and network. Because we want to ensure that as many DMers as possible can afford to participate, attendance is free. We pay for the room and board, and we subsidize travel from distant campuses. Unfortunately, our limited budget has forced us to impose a limit of four students from each campus. We charge additional students who want to attend the Summit as little as possible—$50 for the weekend. In most cases, chapter members divide these additional expenses among themselves, enabling some chapters to bring as many as a dozen members. Our Summits typically attract upward of a hundred DMers as well as staff, board members, and DM alumni/ae.

The three-day Summit weekend falls in late January, right at the beginning of the second semester for most schools. By that time of the academic year, our interns and chapter members had been at work long enough to contribute to and benefit from intense discussions of their organizing experiences—both successes and failures. The Summit taps into these experiences, fostering a process of sharing and mutual learning in small group discussions. The Summit also offers a series of workshops on everything from using the media and running a "great" meeting, to campus publicity ideas, organizing teach-ins, and lobbying elected officials. These are designed to help DM interns and chapter members become more effective organizers.

But learning organizing techniques in the absence of motivating principles is no more satisfactory than a commitment to democracy that does not involve working to achieve it. As a result, we include sessions devoted to the history and theory of democracy. These discussions—sometimes in plenary sessions, sometimes in workshops—explore what an egalitarian political system would look like. Because Jay often leads these sessions, the economics of democracy is frequently the center of attention. Who should pay for the costs involved in candidates running for office? Quite often DMers extend these discussions more widely to other questions—whether there are desirable alternatives to democracy; whether the democracy we envision is utopian; and whether DM's approach to political change is realistic.

We want students to understand that there is no contradiction in DM's promotion of democracy while at the same time acknowledging that we have a specific political agenda. Our commitment to reducing the power of private wealth in the political system defines the organization. But we also seek a wide-ranging, no-holds-barred discussion about all aspects of the organization's agenda.

In all of this we see the Summit as a teaching and learning experience. We designed it on the premise that teachers know more than students about the subject matter at hand, but that no one can be forced to learn. To learn well, individuals have to be motivated. And that motivation is best fostered by encouraging open discussion. Thus an effective learning environment is not one in which a teacher cedes authority, but one in which she or he encourages students to be partners in the learning process. At the Summit we set the agenda and choose the topics to be considered, and at the same time structure an open environment for discussion in order to create a successful learning process.

We are not always successful. Students often resist opening up, at least at first. Most of them have not had much experience with serious discussion. There were times when we simply were unable to break through, unable to overcome a schooling experience largely confined to memorization. In addition, a few of the guest speakers we brought to the Summit have themselves lacked experience with open discussion. There have been occasions when their sessions failed because they only lectured at the students. We tried to deal with this problem by increasingly relying on our own staff rather than on outside "experts." We also enlisted DM alumni and former staff members who better understand the goals and culture of Democracy Matters—one that emphasizes collaboration between students and session leaders.

A related issue that arose in planning the Summit concerned the extent to which we should include "fun" activities in the schedule. The dilemma here is that time is limited and there is much of substance to do. We know that no one can work all of the time. We provide "free time" before dinner, and on Saturday nights after the plenary session we offer a yoga session, music, or a money-and-politics version of popular games. Furthermore, students of course are free to attend whatever sessions they choose. We never take attendance, and if they wish to absent themselves they can do so at their own discretion.

But the fact remains that the Summit is intense and demanding for everyone involved. Over the years there has been some pushback from students about the Summit's level of intensity. Occasionally a complaint will appear among the anonymous conference evaluations to the effect that the Summit was exhausting—with "too many sessions." But this pressure has not been strong enough for us to change. Instead, when we read responses about how inspirational the Summit has been, or come upon a sentence like this one, from a student in 2007, "This stuff is fantastic! At the end I was bursting with energy, ideas, excitement but also a bit burned out," we feel we have struck just about the right balance.

The Summit always begins with a Friday night plenary during which Joan sets the tone for the weekend. She reviews Democracy Matters' origins, history, and purpose. She refers to her own participation in earlier social movements when the power of organized people achieved democratizing reforms. And she points to the fact that DM's student organizing is important at least in part because it continues in that tradition.

Joan's talk has been followed by a presentation by our son Adonal when he was able to grab a few hours from the NBA to be with us. There were times when the schedule of games or his responsibilities as an officer in the NBA Players Association meant he could not attend. But when he does, both his presentation and his presence rivet DMers. After all, Adonal is a celebrity. Few students have ever met or talked with an NBA player, and his openness and personal warmth quickly puts everyone at ease.

Adonal talks about how his college experiences led him to start Democracy Matters. He recounts his annoyance as a student when people claimed that his generation was apathetic, pointing out that students at Colgate and other schools were active in voluntary groups and organizations. These groups provided support for local communities and for causes like the protection of the environment. But he also argues that there were problems. The impact of student groups was compromised by their fragmentation and the lack of communication among them. But most important the groups were marginalized because they avoided politics.

Adonal goes on to describe his vision of creating a new student organization, one that would be non-partisan but political, that can act as a unifying agent among existing campus groups. He expounds on his basic conviction that focusing on a common concern will not only create strong coalitions, but also demonstrate that political engagement will increase the effectiveness of each separate group. He always ends by urging the students to help him fulfill his dream for Democracy Matters: to be so successful in their grassroots organizing that large numbers of college students will finally recognize the enormous potential power they have to help change politics in this country. He wants Democracy Matters to be the catalyst for a social movement that will, as the DM slogan puts it, "get big private money out of politics and people back in." After he concludes, the students always bombard him with questions, sometimes about politics but also about what it is like to play in the NBA. He also tells hilarious stories about what it was like coming to the United States and living with two college professors, whose normal dinnertime conversation included passionate debates about politics.

In the years Adonal did not attend, we invited guest speakers. This was something of a wild card, but among the best of these were four state legislators elected in Maine or Connecticut with public funding. Two of them were under the age of twenty-five, one was a community organizer, and another was a previously homeless person. None of them was wealthy and therefore could not have run for office without public funding. Their discussions of running for office without having to worry about obligations to funders made the issue of money and politics vivid and realistic. They shared their personal stories with the students, and described how being publicly funded legislators meant they could spend time listening to their constituents and responding to their needs. Their testimony was especially important in demonstrating that the kind of reform DM advocates really works. Several challenged the DMers to do even more to pass public financing systems, and all of them encouraged the students to run for office themselves. At their best, these presentations were deeply inspiring, combining personal commitment to social change and experience in organizing.

On a few occasions guest speakers have not been effective. The Summit has a purpose, but that purpose is not well served by dry lectures, nor by presenters who talk more about themselves than about the politics of money. Interestingly, one year the students reacted negatively to a guest speaker in a way we had not anticipated. His presentation emphasized the differences between conservatives and Republicans on the one hand, and liberals and Democrats on the other, who, as groups, took very different positions on the need to reform campaign financing. A few students in the question-and-answer period strongly objected to what they thought was an overly partisan tone. They argued that labels were old-fashioned and inappropriate with regard to campaign finance reform. Their view was that everybody—on the political Right or the political Left, Republican or Democrat—was a potential recruit.

As a frequent presenter at Summit plenaries, Jay encourages students to consider theoretical issues relating to the principles of democracy. He has, for example, talked about the inadequacy of democratic theory when it comes to considering the role of money. His argument is that the political process should be considered as a public good. Candidates should be given financing for their campaigns from tax revenue, as is the case with the defense budget. This would ensure that there is no bias toward funders. At other Summits, citing Wall Street's financial power, he has led lively discussions on how that power has been used to achieve deregulation of the financial sector at the expense of the country as a whole.

A particularly contentious plenary discussion occurred at the 2003 Summit. By then it had become obvious that the Bush administration was planning to invade Iraq. In his presentation, Jay made it clear that he opposed such an intervention, arguing that what lay behind the decision was a flawed energy policy in this country. Behind that policy, in turn, was the political clout that oil and energy firms gain through their campaign contributions. It soon became clear that a considerable number of DMers disagreed, supporting the military intervention in the name of promoting democracy. When this became obvious, Jay had two concerns: that the defenders of the use of the military in Iraq should have adequate time to present their rebuttal to his position, and that the students should discuss the subject with one another in ways consistent with the democratic principle of mutual respect.

As it turned out, the discussion was immensely gratifying. Students sharply questioned Jay and one another concerning the content and strength of the arguments being presented. It was intense, but voices were not raised and interruptions did not occur. Though it did not seem as if many people changed their minds, it was the tone of the debate that was important. It demonstrated that Democracy Matters activists could possess and express strong disagreements while still continuing to work together. One student commented on this in an anonymous Summit evaluation: "I was amazed at how people could be so civilized in their debating. It was wonderful to be with such different people who were all so passionate about the same thing even though they sometimes didn't agree."

At the end, Jay congratulated the group for a discussion that had revealed how serious issues could and should be debated in a democracy of equals. It is this last issue, over and above what the debate meant about Democracy Matters' ability to tolerate diverse opinions that was of importance. The content of a political system is only partially determined by its rules and institutions. Not even the public funding of elections would be enough to ensure a vibrant democracy. The quality of democracy is also determined by the behavior of its participants. We want Democracy Matters students to know how to articulate their points of view persuasively. But we also want them to learn to listen to others' points of view, and be willing when necessary to adjust their own thinking in light of new arguments and information. Such discussion is precisely how a politics of democratic equality will best function. It is a learned behavior. Unfortunately, this form of open political deliberation is all too rare today.

DMers report what they like best at the Summit are its small breakout groups. The very first session on Saturday morning is always the breakout titled "Organizing on Your Campus: First Semester Experiences." Students, all from different campuses, share what they have done, the problems that arose, and the successes they enjoyed. They analyze why some organizing techniques have worked for them while others have not, and brainstorm together about relations with faculty, about recruitment, running meetings, holding events, and much more. Later on the same day, a second breakout session is focused on the future. The same small groups of students meet again, this time to discuss plans for the rest of the year. The specific goal of this breakout session is for DMers to develop ideas and suggestions for Democracy Matters' annual "April Week of Action." During this week, as the culmination of their Spring semester organizing, DM campuses coordinate their activities for five consecutive days. Aside from the Summit itself, nothing is more important in creating a sense of shared participation in important political activism. The best "Week of Action" ideas emerging from the breakouts are presented to the Summit as part of the Saturday evening plenary.

Giving students the opportunity to share their frustrations as well as their successes is one of the most valuable aspects of the Summit. It enables each campus coordinator to place her or his experience in perspective. When openly discussed, coordinators can see that failures are often not the result of an individual organizer's incapacity, but rather rooted in the common characteristics of American politics and university culture.

Our annual summits are not only inspiring for the students, but also for us. The students' anonymous evaluations year after year attest to the positive impact of their coming together with others like themselves to talk about politics. Many are isolated on their campuses, knowing few others who share their passion for change. One participant wrote of the Summit: "This is incredibly important because sometimes I feel helpless and discouraged. We need to bring people together to get them truly motivated." To be surrounded by other young people who are working hard at organizing—despite the difficulties—and by adult activists who have dedicated their lives to political change is a unique experience for them.

Another evaluation captured the tone of the Summit this way: "The Summit got me personally excited and even more determined. It reignited my passion and gave me more information on issues of money in politics. I'm much better equipped to get people active at my school. It was great to learn organizing ideas from other campuses. To be with so many activists in the real sense of the word restores my idealism and hope for change. I'm ready to go back and do more."

CHAPTER 4

CREATING MOMENTUM AND OCCUPY

In 2001–2, the academic year following our successful Colgate pilot, Democracy Matters interns were present on sixteen college campuses in six states—New York, California, North Carolina, Illinois, Connecticut, and Pennsylvania. We had chapters at private and public, urban and rural, large and small, religious, historically black, and secular schools. Among them were some highly selective universities as well as those where competition for admission was not nearly as keen.

As we grew, it became clear that we would have to hire additional staff to help mentor our campus coordinators. We looked for individuals who combined organizing experience and a commitment to our vision of social change. DM field organizers would have to possess the patience and skill of experienced teachers, as well as the ability to relate well to college students.

In the ten years between 2002 and 2012, nineteen field organizers worked with us as links to the campus coordinators. At our peak, we divided responsibilities for mentoring interns among three regional organizers—located in California, Minnesota, and Washington, DC.

Most years however, we were able to fund only one or two field organizing positions. Joan continued to work with students on about a dozen or so campuses each year. Even with her administrative responsibilities, she felt it was important to have direct contact with the heart of the organization.

Becoming a DM field organizer meant taking on an isolated job. Since we could not afford to rent office space, our staff had to work from home. Though the field organizers traveled to visit the campuses they were working with and attended the annual Summit, most of their daily interaction with students, Joan, and one another was by phone or email. For a few staff, particularly those who had recently graduated from colleges where they were surrounded by friends and interacted daily with large numbers of peers, the lack of face-to-face social interaction proved to be too much. As one recently hired staff member explained to Joan in October of 2004, less than two months after she took the job, "I love working with the kids and I hate to quit, but I can't deal with not having a place where I can go to work with other people every day."

Such voluntary departures were rare, however. We were able to hire many talented people, and our best DM field organizers did an absolutely incredible job. Perhaps not surprisingly, four of our best staff members were former Democracy Matters interns who moved into their positions immediately after their graduation. As undergraduate campus coordinators, each had not only successfully built a thriving DM chapter but had demonstrated the talent to motivate younger students who carried on the work. To a person, they all planned to attend graduate or law school to prepare for careers focused on social change and social justice. But like so many other college graduates, they wanted to work for a year or two before going back to school. Democracy Matters field organizing seemed the perfect job. Though each found the transition from college life to a full-time job "bumpy," as one staff member put it, they soon adjusted to the new routine. To Democracy Matters they brought not only knowledge of the role of money in politics and a firsthand understanding of the difficulties of campus organizing but their own experiences in coping with and overcoming those difficulties.

Joan worked closely with each staff member. They were already experienced organizers, but they needed guidance and support to help them through the difficulties they encountered. Since they were geographically dispersed, Joan set up a schedule of daily calls with them. These conversations, often lengthy and wide-ranging, of course included discussion of matters internal to the organization: what the interns were doing, upcoming campus visits, and even fundraising. But they also often dealt with important substantive matters. Changing elections was a means to achieve a greater degree of democracy in society. It was important that staffers understood in-depth the connection between making elections more democratic and making the society more just. Joan came to feel that her discussions with DM field staff constituted an ongoing seminar on politics and social change.

None of our field organizers stayed on for more than three years. We understood their need to move on. The low level of pay we were able offer was only part of the issue. As long as Democracy Matters remained a relatively small organization, we could not provide our staff with career ladders. Soon enough, each of them decided to seek new challenges and growth opportunities. But almost all remained loyal to and involved with Democracy Matters over time—volunteering for our Speakers Bureau, returning for our Annual Summits, serving as board members, or organizing DM fundraising parties with new friends and colleagues.

GROWTH

From its modest beginning of 16 chapters, DM grew rapidly. Between 2004 and 2008 we had interns on as many as 80 campuses. In recent years that number has dropped somewhat. Even so, DM still maintains a presence on between 40 and 50 campuses each year.

We have never found a foolproof method for selecting campus coordinators and probably never will. In reality, organizing is not a science but an art. People with remarkably different personalities and experiences can become effective political organizers. This is the reason we took chances in our hiring of interns. What we were looking for with every single candidate were the often subtle clues that indicated the presence of both commitment and charisma that would make success likely.

Each year we often chose right; but sometimes we chose wrong. With regard to the wrong choices, the annual pattern was that three or four students would resign from their internships very early in the Fall semester. Some had underestimated the demands of their schoolwork, and others found themselves faced with family financial or health problems requiring them to find additional jobs or spend time at home. And there were students who came to realize that they had taken on a more difficult task than they had anticipated, one to which they could not do justice.

In other cases we were the ones who took action to dismiss interns. This decision would be made by Joan in collaboration with the field organizers, requiring that we be clear on what we thought constituted success and failure. How should we evaluate the work of the campus coordinators? We did have some ostensibly "objective" criteria for evaluation. Interns were required to report weekly to an assigned field organizer. Close collaboration between Democracy Matters staff and campus coordinators was integral to our model of political organizing. Coordinators discussed what had happened in the previous week and what they were planning in the future. In addition, interns were also required to complete at least four projects or campaigns each semester. Failure to fulfill these requirements led to probation and sometimes withdrawal of the internship.

The penalty for missing the mandated weekly discussion between staff and interns was straightforward: if it did not occur the internship was put at risk. But the nature and scope of the students' projects varied considerably and was more difficult to evaluate. Was publishing an article about public campaign financing in the school paper the equivalent of organizing a teach-in? When an inexperienced intern on a politically conservative campus held a pizza and politics discussion attended by only three students should that count as successful? Was it a success when a second-year intern secured a hundred signatures on a petition at a school with an active political culture? How should the staff decide what success looked like and who was doing enough?

It was impossible to have one criterion against which to measure everyone. Each campus and each intern was unique. Field organizers could not possibly expect the same level of success from an intern with no previous political experience as they did from one who had done this kind of work before. Similarly, an intern organizing on a small campus with a cooperative administration and a history of campus activism could be expected to get much better results than a campus coordinator trying to start a chapter at a huge university where the administration was less than supportive of student organizations.

Instead of a rigid standard of evaluation, we trained our staff to judge the extent of the intern's effort. We judged input more than output. We were looking for effort and improvement. Both could be evaluated with the information obtained from campus visits and from weekly staff conversations. On this basis we were able to make separate judgments for each intern. Success, then was measured by standards relevant to each intern and campus, and with an understanding of the difficulty of what the intern was trying to accomplish.

Each year about a quarter of our DM chapters had to be considered failures. Sometimes, as noted, students resigned because of personal problems or too much schoolwork. But over the years resignations have increasingly occurred due to the mounting financial pressures students are experiencing. As student loan debt grows, those who otherwise would be available to do an internship at minimal pay are forced to turn to part-time employment to help pay the bills. Since the 2008 recession the number of individuals who could not accept an internship or have been forced to give it up because of economic pressures has grown. In addition, in contrast to the enthusiasm with which Barack Obama's 2008 election was greeted by students, some interns resigned as a result of their disillusionment as the luster of his first campaign faded.

There were also situations in which Joan and the staff decided to withdraw an internship because the campus coordinator was simply not doing the job. Some coordinators turned out to be too assertive or rigid, while others were too timid to even try to organize. Although we tried to address personal issues that interfered with organizing and worked hard to help such students, the fact is that some of what it takes to be a good organizer simply cannot be taught. When we found that a student was out of his or her depth, we thought it best for both sides to terminate the relationship.

Even on successful campuses, our staff was often frustrated as students struggled to find a balance between their DM responsibilities and other demands on their time. Interns faced pressure from their schoolwork, from their involvement with other campus groups, and from friends and family. We were constantly competing with activities that pulled students in different directions at once.

An important factor that affected the success or failure of DM chapters was the culture of the school where our interns were working —something over which we had no control. Some universities with long traditions of activism had so much going on that as a new organization Democracy Matters had great difficulty breaking in. Yet on other campuses a culture of activism seemed to benefit our organizing efforts. Other determinants were equally unpredictable. Neither the size nor location of the school, the level of faculty support, nor the presence of fraternities and sororities seemed to predict DM failure or success. What we can say at best is that though some DMers had success, others struggled, and it did not matter much whether the school was large or small, urban or rural, public or private.

Some aspects of political DM organizing proved especially difficult for almost all of our interns. The prospect of reaching out to off-campus local groups—whether high school students, civic associations, political activists, or elected officials—was daunting. Doing so was made difficult because such groups and individuals often failed to respond positively when our students approached them. But it was also the case that the DMers were hesitant to reach out. They told their field organizers that they felt more confident and secure dealing with their peers or even with their own faculty and administrators. They were intimidated by the idea of doing political organizing off-campus. Very few interns or DM chapter members followed up on our suggestion to reach out to people at home during vacations. We asked them to visit their former high schools and make presentations to classes. Similarly, we encouraged them to speak at civic associations or local organizations and to ask their parents and relatives to sign up for our *E-News* or to contribute financially to Democracy Matters. But as far as we know, almost none of this happened.

DMers generally can be characterized as unaffiliated, left-of-center individuals. They take the idea of American democracy seriously and are dismayed that wealth distorts that process. Most are sympathetic to environmental and other single-issue movements, but do not see themselves as activists within them. Although they certainly have more of an affinity with the Democratic Party than Republican, they are critical of both. They tend to believe that there is too much inequality in the country's distribution of income and wealth, but they do not possess a principled animus to a market economy. In short, we have attracted "democrats"—largely non-ideological and politically inexperienced but idealistic young people who otherwise would not have a political home. Our coordinators and campus chapters do not possess the hard edge of students who are more ideologically driven nor the despair of those who have endured the frustrations of repeated political defeats.

These characteristics on the whole serve the organization well. As revealed in our 2003 Summit debate on Iraq, Democracy Matters is an open and tolerant place. But that same lack of aggressiveness sometimes shows up as a tendency toward a self-effacing, least-common-denominator brand of politics that, left unchecked, mutes our message. Such a reluctance to be hard-edged often reveals itself when DM chapters co-sponsor events with other campus groups. When this happens, we want DMers to strongly articulate the need for public funding and in the process become the glue that ties campus organizations together. But the fact is that in these contexts DMers too often fail to assert the coalition leadership role they could take. These same students in other contexts are highly articulate as they forcefully point out the distortions in politics caused by the role of private wealth. Their failure to take the political lead when in coalition, then, is not caused by a lack of commitment to the issue; rather, it is their reluctance to appear too aggressive. As Frank, a DM intern at Notre Dame, wrote: "I was afraid when I started that if I was too political I would scare off students. I held back and was kind of quiet, but after a while I learned that that doesn't get you anywhere." Politically inexperienced students like Frank often worry about raising the issue of public campaign financing in contexts in which it might not fit easily or might be offensive to some.

Certainly that problem would have been much less in evidence if Democracy Matters had attracted more ideologically driven students or those with prior political experience. But if we had, the tone and tenor of the organization would have been very different. With a more politically experienced membership, Democracy Matters would, to be sure, have been a more sophisticated organization. Reluctance to aggressively push our own agenda probably would not have been a problem. But there would be a price to be paid as well— the disappearance of the feel of Democracy Matters as a politically engaged but open and idealistic group.

This friendly and accommodating ambiance has on the whole been beneficial. Because of it, DMers can overcome the suspicion and hostility toward politics expressed by most college students. DMers can relate well to the concerns and ideas of students who, though insisting they are apolitical, nonetheless worry about the world around them. It also has been central to our ability to manage disagreements within the organization.

OCCUPY

The appearance of Occupy Wall Street in the Fall of 2011 was a galvanizing experience for Democracy Matters. Initially wary of Occupy's activism, DMers quickly came to see direct action and Occupy's encampments as a particularly dramatic vehicle for the articulation of their own political aspirations. For DM chapters, the existence of Occupy produced a level of energy and activity that surpassed anything in our previous experience. If Occupy Wall Street had survived, it might have provided a continuing impetus for DM's growth. Occupy opened up the issue of inequality for debate on campuses. And DM's emphasis on reducing the political influence of the wealthy donor class provided a mechanism to achieve Occupy's goal of greater equality. Occupy Wall Street vividly dramatized the issues that animated DMers.

Until Occupy took to the streets, political and economic inequality had not been the trigger for large organized protests—indeed, the topic was rarely part of the ongoing political dialogue in the mainstream of American politics. But as Occupy Wall Street demonstrations and activism caught the attention of the country, anger at the concentration of wealth symbolized by Wall Street financial institutions and the power their wealth allowed them to exercise over elections and politics became the focus of political discussion. This occurred nowhere more than on college campuses.

Democracy Matters chapters did not participate in the first Occupy Wall Street activities in New York City. We like others had failed to anticipate its advent. But as Occupy spread onto college campuses, DMers eagerly joined in. The connections between Occupy's issues and our own were obvious. The political clout possessed by campaign donors, especially those in the financial sector, had clearly played a critical role in the growth of economic inequality. DMers argued that Occupy had placed a problem on the national agenda that to be corrected required campaign finance reform legislation.

The stir created by Occupy Wall Street played to DM's advantage. Our message seemed more relevant than in the past. Inequality and corporate money in politics had become the topic of frequent conversations and coverage by national media. The impact on our campus chapters was striking: meetings increased in frequency and were better attended; more events were planned; school newspapers solicited Democracy Matters' views; and the demand for DM presentations increased. When we spoke on campuses that fall, we had larger audiences than in the past. The events were often electric, with students questioning and debating inequality, money in politics, and the meaning of activism, social movements, and social change.

The partnership forged between new Occupy Wall Street groups and DM chapters helped both movements. Because Democracy Matters on many campuses had already established itself as an official organization and was able to reserve rooms and post flyers, it could facilitate Occupy's organizing. At the same time, Occupy Wall Street had touched a nerve among young people—previously inactive students were now energized. Democracy Matters benefited from this heightened level of activity. DMers were prominent as speakers and participants at many Occupy events. With DM's unambiguous stance in favor of public funding for election campaigns and its link to political inequality, DM campus chapters were delivering a convincing message to receptive ears.

It is true that the Occupy Wall Street protests dissipated within several months. Nevertheless the protests had revealed the existence of a large cohort of students and others who, frustrated by the dominance of wealth in American society, wanted collectively to push back. In this, DMers found kindred spirits. They saw that they were not alone in their dissatisfaction with the status quo. Just as important, they were able to observe, for the first time in their lives, the power of direct action to focus the entire society's attention on a previously ignored social problem. At the same time, DMers were forced to confront the basic conundrum that faces all protest politics: How much should they rely on direct action as opposed to participating in conventional institutionalized politics? In light of what Occupy had accomplished, as well as its limitations, DMers had to decide for themselves what they thought the appropriate balance should be.

Establishing that balance was the source of DM's political differences with Occupy Wall Street. Occupy's official statements and its practice made one thing crystal clear. Occupy was not interested in reforming the political system. David Graeber, the author of the slogan "We are the 99 percent" and an influential voice in the Occupy movement, wrote that Occupy Wall Street refuses "to recognize the legitimacy of existing political institutions." For Occupy, it was a matter of principle that it not issue demands. Doing so, Graeber wrote, "means recognizing the legitimacy—or at least the power—of those of whom the demands are made." Instead, Occupy engaged in direct action "acting as if the existing structure of power does not even exist."[16]

The difference in political outlook between Occupy Wall Street and Democracy Matters was stark. Democracy Matters provides a home for students who believe the electoral system has to be reformed and can be made more democratic. They do not question its legitimacy, and most believe that acting as if it does not exist would be an artifice that impairs the probability of success. Occupy's criticisms of inequality were attractive to DMers, but that movement's estrangement from the political process was not. There was, in short, an overlapping concern over objectives, but also a profound divergence concerning the political process.

The 2011 DM Summit featured an intense discussion about Occupy. Not surprisingly there were differences of opinion on the subject. Basic political issues were at stake. No one present argued that we should follow Occupy's lead and give up entirely on the political system. But there were some DMers who thought that Occupy

Wall Street's success demonstrated that we had been too tame: we were not aggressive enough nor sufficiently in the streets. Others countered that shifting to more direct action would be self-defeating. In fact they argued that not many students had actually participated in Occupy's actions. They maintained that a shift in DM's tactics would foreclose our ability to persuade the uncommitted.

As in 2003 when Iraq was the subject of debate, DMers attending the Summit were able to articulate strong disagreements without putting the organization at risk. The issues were fully aired without necessarily changing minds. What emerged was a consensus that there was organizational room for those who wanted to engage in more direct action as well as for those who did not. There would be no single Democracy Matters position. Each chapter could determine its own strategy.

As was also the case in 2003, we were entirely comfortable with this outcome. We liked the fact that the range of tactics available to activists had been fully debated. We approved of the tone of the discussion, respectful and serious, with no ad hominum attacks. We also thought that, politically, open-endedness was the appropriate stance for the organization to take. Political diversity characterizes Democracy Matters. It therefore makes sense that tactical diversity mirrors the differences within the organization.

It was also clear to us that something other than the choice of organizational strategy was under way in our debates. In the microcosm of Democracy Matters, the debate was a learning experience in democratic practice. It was an event that would influence the students in attendance as they become adults and participants in the country's political process. In a country in which right-wing talk radio has encouraged rhetorical excess, the young people at the DM Summit were experiencing a different model of political discourse: deliberation took the place of denunciation; rational argument replaced rhetorical excess; evidence was required; and conspiracies were doubted. That the discussion was intellectually gratifying as well as producing a sound strategy for the organization left us thinking that we had advanced the practice of democracy. It was not simply that we were attempting to reduce the role of private money in politics. We were also helping young people to learn how to participate in an open democratic system.

CHAPTER 5

PROBLEMS OF MOVEMENT BUILDING

Social movements are "vast and somewhat unstructured endeavors whose participants express new ways of thinking and agitate for institutional transformation," according to Theda Skocpol, a prominent Harvard University sociologist. She writes that the social movements of the 1960s and early 1970s "synthesized grassroots protest, activist radicalism, and professionally led efforts to lobby government and educate the public." The movements mobilized large numbers of activist participants with the intention of moving incumbent politicians to legislate reform and to create conditions that would enable reform-minded politicians to ascend to office. Most important, from our perspective, was the role played by students. As Skocpol puts it, "At the forefront of these groundswells were younger Americans, especially from the growing ranks of college students and university graduates."[17] The Civil Rights Act of 1964 and the Voting Rights Act of 1965 stand as examples of the successes that can be achieved by social movements.

With this history in mind, we hoped that Democracy Matters would contribute to the creation of a movement that would democratize the country's political system. But by the time Democracy

Matters got under way, the era of social movements had crested. In place of social movements, "protest as a strategy was overtaken by policy advocacy," Skocpol writes. The dominant vehicle for progressive politics had become professionally staffed organizations, typically based in Washington, DC, or New York. Instead of grassroots organizing, the emphasis shifted to lobbying, pursuing litigation, and issuing reports based on in-house research. Mobilizing large numbers of citizens for rallies and demonstrations of the kind that characterized the earlier era was not part of the new approach. Skocpol describes the new organizations as "practicing politics in much the same way as the business and professional lobbies against which they often square off in policy disputes."[18]

Why progressives shifted from movement-building to policy advocacy is not entirely clear. But almost certainly the emergence of what J. Craig Jenkins has called "social movement philanthropy" played a part in the transition.[19] Philanthropic grants to social movement–type organizations skyrocketed during the same years that grassroots mobilizations declined, and the new organizational model became dominant. The dollar value of "social philanthropy grants"— foundation grants to independent organizations seeking institutional change—in inflation-adjusted dollars increased from under $4 million in 1967 to $16 million in 1977. Significantly, only a tiny percentage of these grants went to student organizations: 0.35 percent of the funds dispersed.

Jenkins writes, "Professionalization has been the most direct impact of movement philanthropy." He believes that foundations contribute "little to grassroots participation" and "have also shunned movements that operate in contentious areas, such as international peace and poverty." Their increased financial role changed the environment in which movement politics was practiced. In addition, there is evidence that "foundation patronage has reduced the incentives for movement leaders to pursue indigenous organizing and thus indirectly weakened the movements."

Building a grassroots student movement for campaign finance reform is an expensive undertaking. As our Democracy Matter experience illustrates, it is a labor-intensive project. Even at the minimum level we were able to afford, DM's wage bill (for the executive director, field staff, and campus coordinators) was far and away our largest cost item. The same would be true if a larger social movement actually did get under way. It would not have to match what the opposition, in all likelihood, would be able to spend. But it is clear that it would take a lot of money to mobilize numbers against wealth.

Though Adonal had been very generous in providing us with financial viability, scaling up in the way necessary to achieve our movement-building hopes required raising much more money than he had available. Furthermore, we knew that, like other athletes, his years as a professional were limited. We would have to go outside of Democracy Matters to become adequately financed. Although Adonal's initial commitment provided us with the resources to get started, we would require more funds to have the impact we hoped for.

In response, we built a list of supporters to whom we sent appeals. We communicated with and re-solicited them over the years. But the contributions we received from this source did not come close to meeting our needs. Our only alternative was to turn to wealthy individuals and foundations for support. The problem, however, was that with the exception of Adonal, none of us knew anyone who was really wealthy. Aware that other organizations working on campaign finance reform received foundation grants, we set to work to implement a foundation fundraising plan.

With this in mind, we applied to every foundation that included deepening democracy or building civic engagement in their mission statement. We wrote letters of inquiry, called program officers, and made as many appointments as possible to meet with them. We hired a professional filmmaker to create a DM video featuring our students, printed other materials to send to foundations, wrote lengthy proposals, and enlisted Joan and Adonal to carry out the plan.

The argument we made to foundation program officers was that we were laying the groundwork for a future social movement. For such a movement to emerge, it was necessary to train and encourage a new generation of effective political organizers. This in turn required close mentoring and training of young people—especially college students. Social movements are created only over relatively long periods of time, during which there are very likely to be protracted periods of stagnation when they will not make much progress. Ours, therefore, was an educational project that would come to fruition only after extensive preparation.

Our efforts to secure financing from philanthropic organizations strongly confirm Jenkins's analysis of foundation funding. They are not interested in supporting either college students or grassroots social movements. With the exception of a couple of foundations that provided us with small one-year start-up grants, it was soon clear that our emphasis on the grassroots and college students put us at cross-purposes with the foundation world's commitments.

Illustrative of the mismatch between ourselves and foundations was the difficulty we encountered in providing "evidence" that would satisfy them concerning our effectiveness. We could provide data on the number of students who had become committed DM activists and the number of events they organized, classes they spoke in, neighborhoods they canvassed, and students and faculty they reached. All of this was in the service of building a movement that sometime in the future might exert enough pressure to achieve reform. But none of this data represented the kind of "measurables" that foundations sought. They wanted to know how many votes in Congress had been secured and how our efforts had moved the reform process closer to victory in the current legislative session. They sought immediate and concrete results in the political system. What we could deliver was not of interest to them, and what foundations wanted we could not deliver. We believe that reforming the funding basis of American politics can only be achieved with broad popular pressure. In contrast, virtually without exception, foundation funders do not see a social movement as the prerequisite for change.

Even those foundations most committed to social change found movement-building daunting. In one memorable conversation, a lengthy and mutually stimulating discussion of social change and social movements, the program officer of a major foundation concluded by saying how sorry she was that she could offer no financial support. She genuinely respected what Democracy Matters was doing. She urged us to come back with a proposal in "a few years" when we had built the movement and could demonstrate our effectiveness in actually securing the reforms we sought. The fact that there could be no movement-building without significant financial resources from her foundation seemed to be as lost on her as it was on many otherwise sympathetic foundation representatives with whom we spoke.

Aside from this disagreement about the means necessary to achieve reform, another issue results in foundations' incapacity to act as movement-builders. They see themselves as investors, providing the initial resources to help their grantees get off the ground. They do not expect the non-profits they subsidize will literally become income-generating entities. Rather, the model that they have in mind is that a successful organization will use an initial short-term grant to become attractive to other potential donors.

Given the political nature of our project this approach is a dead-end. DM's funding base is necessarily narrow. It is not possible to foresee a situation in which we could become self-sufficient in the sense of possessing an extensive funding base. Seeing this, almost all foundations rejected our appeals.

We did, however, receive small start-up grants from the Ford Foundation, the Open Society Institute, and the Carnegie Corporation. But these start-up funds were available only for a limited time.[20] When it became clear that we could not count on much foundation support, we were forced to limit our expansion. As a result, our growth trajectory was slower than it otherwise could have been.

Another perverse characteristic of the foundation world creates organizational problems, especially for long-term movement-building. Foundations are organizations that are in a constant state of reevaluation. There are years in which they stop making grants or at least sharply limit them in order to undertake lengthy periods of rethinking and redefinition—in their jargon, " strategic planning." The outcome of that rethinking is a great deal of churning in programs and grant-making. A new strategic plan often results in the disappearance of established programs, to be replaced by new ones that in time are discarded as well.

When Democracy Matters first entered the world of campaign finance reform, most of the funding available was concentrated in a few states where there was thought to be a chance of passing full public financing of election campaigns. Then, around 2005, most foundation funding for campaign finance efforts shifted focus. Grants for state reform dried up and foundation resources were primarily awarded to organizations working in Washington to pass national congressional public financing. In another example, though full public funding of electoral campaigns like those implemented in Maine and Arizona was the political objective supported by foundations for a number of years, that goal was replaced by the objective of promoting "small donor" public financing in a matching funds system.[21]

The instability that emanated from the foundation world affected all the organizations that were part of the campaign finance reform community. Foundations exerted constant pressure to redefine and revise projects, at least formally, so as to match their new qualifications. Much creative effort went into choosing language that would allow organizations to be true to their own goals, yet at the same time match the new requirements imposed by foundations. Not only did this involve a waste of time, there was a political price to be paid as well. Some projects that were effective and worthwhile had to be abandoned for lack of funds, with talented staff let go because their skills were no longer required. Furthermore, the frequent need to adjust and readjust meant that goals often became clouded and the political impact of projects built up over time was squandered.

We consciously made the decision not to participate in the game of following the foundation lead. We would stick to our project and not spend time trying to redefine what we did to fit the latest foundation fashion. Undoubtedly, this decision was costly. For example, one foundation wanted us to no longer concentrate on a "process" issue like money in politics, but to expand by organizing around the environment. Before the 2008 election, another offered us a large grant to register college students to vote. In the first case we argued in response that progress on environmental protection and climate change was improbable unless and until elected officials were freed from dependence on campaign funding from the energy industry. The funder was not convinced and refused to renew our grant. And in the other example, we agreed to do voter registration. But we would do so only as part of an overall strategy to build a movement in support of campaign finance reform. We never got that grant either.

All of this came down to a fundamental political disagreement. We believed that progressive political change required the building of a mass movement in which young people would play an important role. In contrast, most foundations did not believe that it was necessary to fund long-term movement-building. They remained unpersuaded that they should provide resources to assist college students in becoming politically active. In these and other instances, we chose to continue to do what we thought would be most effective in creating political change, even if it meant doing so on a smaller scale than we had hoped.

ADULT REFORM ORGANIZATIONS

At the time Democracy Matters was founded, two major national citizen organizations led the effort for campaign finance reform,

Common Cause and Public Campaign. Both were structured as advocacy organizations. Neither concentrated on building a social movement to attain its objectives. There would be no huge rallies in Washington or elsewhere in the country, such as those that propelled the civil rights movement, the opposition to the war in Vietnam, or the pro-choice movement. Instead, Common Cause's model was, as Andrew McFarland puts it, to place their lobbying efforts "in the hands of hard-hitting experts," professionals based both in Washington and in a number of state capitals. According to McFarland, the belief was that lobbying by professionals with technical expertise would be more effective than that of "naïve and moralistic volunteers who couldn't compete with hardened politicians and other lobbyists."[22] The same pattern was present with Public Campaign, formed in 1997. It was a smaller organization than Common Cause and, unlike the latter's broad agenda, it concentrated its efforts on the single objective of achieving the full public financing of election campaigns. But Public Campaign did not create its own state chapters, instead it forged alliances with already existing organizations in order to promote campaigns to win public financing.

Joan had worked with Common Cause in the late 1990s at both the national and state levels, organizing public campaign-financing campaigns in Oakland and San Francisco. In 2000, Public Campaign and its staff had already helped to pass, implement, and defend full public financing in both Maine and Arizona. Seeking advice based on its experiences in winning public campaign financing, Joan had spoken frequently with the staff of Public Campaign while organizing in California.

When we started Democracy Matters, we were eager to collaborate with both of these organizations. We thought that doing so would be mutually beneficial. On the one hand, interaction between Democracy Matters student activists and the staff and volunteers of adult-based organizations throughout the country could provide important support for the work of our chapters. Both Public Campaign and Common Cause were respected organizations composed of experienced political activists. There was a lot they could teach our students. Working in coalition with these organizations and getting to know such people would provide an invaluable opportunity for DMers to learn about the breadth and seriousness of efforts at campaign finance reform. It could also expose them to people who had chosen political activism as their life's work. They would be in touch with adult mentors and role models, relationships that few if any of them had previously experienced. Furthermore, having on-the-ground adult activists nearby to whom Democracy Matters chapters could relate, and to a certain extent rely on, would supplement our own staff's support. Building alliances with these national organizations would also likely help us—as a new organization—to become part of the broader world of campaign finance reform.

But it was not just Democracy Matters that would benefit. We were confident that such relationships would work because Democracy Matters too had a great deal to offer. We could contribute in unique ways to the strength and effectiveness of adult-based reform efforts. That student activism in the past had been an important source of creativity, idealism, and energy in social movements was not in doubt. DMers could also make such a contribution to state and local efforts at campaign finance reform. Furthermore, both of these organizations had rapidly aging memberships. They worried about, but had not had much success in, attracting young members. Democracy Matters presented an opportunity to include a fresh cohort of experienced young people. Forging relationships across generations was sure to energize both adult groups.

Once Democracy Matters was up and running in 2001, we were eagerly welcomed as an ally in the fight for campaign finance reform. The leaders of both Common Cause and Public Campaign assured us that they understood young people to be an important but neglected constituency. But aside from our becoming a recognized organization within the reform community, very little cooperation actually emerged. With only a few scattered exceptions, we were not able to get either of these organizations to work with us in a way that could produce the mutually beneficial outcomes we had hoped for. We were only formal allies.

As was the case in our relations with foundations, the problem was political. Both Common Cause and Public Campaign were DC-based professional advocacy groups, not movement builders. They did not believe that student activism would be effective in their "inside" strategy of convincing legislators to pass reform. They often talked about how exciting it was to have students working on the issue. But their *modus operandi* left no room for movement-building or student activism. In important ways the inside strategy favored by our allies stands in opposition to the social movement approach we advocate. One depends upon the power that local organized constituencies generate. The other depends on persuading elected officials with argumentation.

CHAPTER 6

APOLITICAL UNIVERSITIES

As faculty members, we understand and endorse the principle that colleges and universities are institutions that should be politically and ideologically neutral. All points of view must be welcomed; debate should be free; staffing and admissions should not involve tests of belief. These are values that go to the core of higher education and should not be violated.

It is within such a commitment to free deliberation that we place Democracy Matters. Our role is to provide one among many outlets for students. DM is not part of the curriculum. It is an extracurricular activity available to students who believe in its principles. Obviously not every student agrees with DM, and no one is obligated to join. But at the same time, it is in the spirit of free association and dialogue that it, like other political organizations, should be welcomed on campus. The presence of groups like Democracy Matters not only provides a political outlet for interested students. It enriches the intellectual life of a university community.

In principle this perspective is widely accepted among academics. Only a few colleges, largely among those dominated by theological doctrines, find these principles untenable. In fact, most institutions of higher education in the United States not only endorse extracurricular campus activities but also establish support mechanisms that encourage student participation in them. With a wide latitude of acceptance, both faculty and administrators agree that students not only should be allowed, but encouraged to pursue their interests and talents on campus and outside of the classroom. Our experience, however, suggests that in practice what goes on falls far short of what is implied by this formal commitment.

When we first envisioned Democracy Matters, we were confident that we would be able to work with and receive assistance from university programs designed to promote and increase citizen engagement and community service. These programs had grown rapidly on college campuses, and by the time of DM's founding they represented an important component of students' university experience. Research indicates that over the course of their higher education careers, most students engage in volunteer services, particularly tutoring and mentoring.[23] Offices that promote student volunteerism and civic engagement typically have broad mission statements that ostensibly seem to include—or at least not exclude—efforts to influence public policy. These statements almost always contain language to suggest that, by encouraging community service, their programs are designed to help students become civic and political leaders and agents of change in the future.

A number of national organizations and projects have supported these university efforts. In 2003, for example, the American Association of State Colleges and Universities (AASCU), in partnership with the *New York Times*, created what they called the American

Democracy Project (ADP). Its mission was to assist public institutions of higher education in "preparing the next generation of informed, engaged citizens for our democracy." [24] Another example is the American Association of Colleges and Universities (AAC&U). This well-established organization works with institutions of higher learning to make "liberal learning an influence on educational practice and institutional purpose . . . [by] creating models for engaging diversity, democracy, interdependence, inequalities, and societal challenges in all students' learning."[25] Still another organization promoting civic engagement is Campus Compact (CC), founded in 1985 by a group of university presidents to promote "community service, civic engagement, and service-learning in higher education" in order to develop "students' citizenship skills."[26] With its strong ties to government programs like Vista, its extensive network of state and national offices, and the support of prominent foundations, Campus Compact is present at schools throughout the country.

The federal government has also weighed in. The Department of Education commissioned a number of reports and studies exploring how to increase college students' engagement in democracy. In January 2012, it released two such documents—"A Crucible Moment: College Learning and Democracy's Future" and "Civil Learning and Engagement in Democracy: A Road Map and Call to Action." Secretary of Education Arne Duncan marked the occasion by stating: "Today's students are tomorrow's leaders, and giving them a strong foundation in civic values is critical to the vitality of America's democracy." [27]

Because of the language used by such organizations, we believed there to be considerable overlap between our own vision and activities and theirs. We thought they would welcome a collaborative relationship with Democracy Matters. After all, there could be no doubt that Democracy Matters aspired to train the political change agents of the future.

Initially, Joan developed a personal relationship with several of the national groups supporting college students' engagement. She was invited to speak and present workshops at early ADP conferences, and to write for their newsletter. In turn, she sent DM information to lists of ADP faculty and administrators. She had several conversations with the director of the AAC&U, and spoke at a number of Campus Compact state meetings.

But collaboration did not go much further than that. For example, though Campus Compact's Vista volunteers at many campuses were sympathetic when DMers approached them seeking to work together, they always explained that they were legally barred from working with political organizations, even nonpartisan ones like Democracy Matters. Though DM students did join a few ADP-sponsored projects like campus voter-registration drives, these collaborations generally never went very far, and certainly never became the basis for a coalition calling for campaign finance reform.

In failing to join with us, these organizations missed the opportunity to provide their students with experiences that would help them develop important citizenship skills—which was precisely their ostensible objective. But in our case the skills developed would be those required to work effectively in the political process. These skills are of value: they are important in a democracy and, in our judgment, are in short supply in this country. Instead of teaching students how to influence the political process, what these national organizations offered were social service activities. While exposing young people to the flaws in our society, they do nothing to help them learn how to work at a system level to correct those shortcomings. A recent list of "program models" on Campus Compact's website included such anodyne activities as student volunteers collecting contributions for food pantries and teaming up with elementary schools for a day of service. Other non-controversial and decidedly apolitical events promoted were "a fun-filled children's literacy event, a homecoming week Habitat for Humanity event, and developing a caring intergeneration link."[28]

Our frustrating experience with these programs as representative has been established by recent research on the subject. Anne Colby and her associates have documented the absence of political options for student volunteers. They note that "students are offered a great wealth of opportunities to do community service, but they perceive very few opportunities and little encouragement to become politically involved." The report notes that among six hundred such programs, only one percent "included a focus on specifically political concerns and solutions."[29]

It seems that the theory at work in encouraging volunteerism and civic engagement in institutions of higher education has two components. The first is that the volunteers will develop a heightened concern for the disadvantaged. The second, left unstated but clearly implied, is that on the basis of these non-political activities, students will go on to become advocates on behalf of those they volunteered to help. To be advocates for changed policies is necessarily to be political, and that is what the defenders of civic engagement seem to mean when they claim that the kind of volunteerism they promote will strengthen democracy.

There is however a great deal of evidence suggesting that these programs do not work in that way. Citing William A. Galston's survey work, Jon Dalton and Pamela Crosby write that "despite the many positive student outcomes that community service promotes, it does not appear to guarantee students' active involvement in the political process." Indeed, they argue, volunteerism may have a "negative impact on political engagement by channeling some youth away and offering them a satisfying alternative to political participation."[30] These programs, in short, do not encourage the volunteers to move beyond their own moral development. As if to confirm the anti-political impact of university volunteerism, the Dalton and Crosby study quotes a student who flatly states: "I don't do politics, but my service work is political."[31]

By avoiding political activities, the programs provide no linkage between students' observing deprivation and their actually becoming agents of change. Student volunteers may observe social injustice or systematic exploitation and discrimination. But they are not instructed how to work politically to overcome it or even provided with the opportunity to engage in politics.

There is no doubt that when students provide health, educational, and legal services to the needy, good work is being done. But the belief that contact with the needs of the people they are working with will necessarily move students to political engagement is a profound *non sequitur*. Political activism requires exposure to and experience with the political process. Without it, even the best-intentioned will lack the knowledge and skills necessary to function effectively in that forum as active citizens.

We can do no more than speculate about the reasons that campus-based civic engagement offices eschew politics. But our conjecture is that their administrators worry that student political activism would offend local organizations and university supporters. This in all likelihood is more of an issue at public than at private universities. Indeed, several administrators at state universities confirmed to us that they consciously shied away from controversy in order to avoid a backlash. They confided that because their university depended on legislators for funding, they took great care to avoid campus activities that might be construed as political. Though private universities are less dependent upon officeholders, they too receive federal and state funds. In addition, they require donations from alumni and other private contributors. Thus private schools also have an incentive to avoid having their students involved in anything that might seem contentious. Furthermore—perhaps because memories of the 1960s have not yet faded—it is likely that in order to not scare off the parents of prospective students, colleges and universities seek to avoid the potentially negative national publicity that has often accompanied student political activism.

The bottom line here is that though universities often articulate the desire to educate students for citizenship, the programs they support almost invariably exclude the kind of political activism that Democracy Matters encourages. We are much more political than the typical campus-based community service and civic engagement projects. While there may be some overlap, and despite our non-partisanship, it is clear that we differ in fundamental ways.

CAMPUS RULES

Every university has an administrative office that oversees student life. These offices formulate and enforce a set of rules governing student clubs and organizations. Although on some campuses the personnel working in these offices have provided genuine help to our DM chapters, our interns' experience with them has been overwhelmingly negative. DMers consistently met with difficulties when interacting with these offices. It is unclear to us why university administrations have developed complex sets of rules and requirements for student groups. It may be an effort to stymie activism, perhaps in response to threatening echoes of the 1960s. Alternatively it might be a preemptive attempt to defend their university against possible legal action or the withdrawal of financial support. A third possibility is that administrators simply want exercise authoritative control over the young people on their campuses. Regardless of their motivation, however, the fact is that though these offices claim to facilitate campus activities, Democracy Matters interns—almost without exception—have found them to be at best unresponsive and at worst impediments.

Very few colleges or universities give their students the freedom to initiate and engage in any organizational activities without satisfying a lengthy list of requirements. On the contrary, the vast majority insists that undergraduates adhere to a strict set of bureaucratic rules. Taken as a whole, these regulations make it difficult and sometimes impossible for students to set up clubs or to engage in perfectly reasonable activities of their own choosing.

Most problematic in this regard is the Catch-22 requirement that students obtain official permission or recognition prior to initiating any organizational function. Undergraduates are prevented from handing out leaflets, putting up posters, reserving rooms, or organizing informational meetings and events until their "club" is officially recognized by the school. It does not take a Yossarian to realize that those precisely are the activities that are necessary to attract people to form a group in the first place. Illustrative was Janeen's experience at Sonoma State University in California. Throughout the year she constantly complained to her DM field organizer about her difficulties with her school's Student Activities office. In her end-of-semester report, she exploded, "How can they expect us to attract enough students to get recognition or require us to 'show that we are serious' when they won't let us DO anything—we can't even put up a sign for a general interest meeting. It's nuts!"

Requirements for recognition vary widely from university to university. Most obligate students to submit a constitution, obtain a specified number of signatures from students who agree to join the organization, and to fill officer positions. Many withhold recognition until students can secure a faculty advisor. Mandatory attendance of club officers at lengthy administration-led meetings during the year is common, as are requirements to specify the goals of the organization, the club's justification for existence, and evidence that its mission does not overlap with any other campus group. Some schools even insist that students raise a specified amount of money for their club from other students before it can be granted recognition. Others enforce the automatic delay of a semester before according a club full official status.

Democracy Matters campus coordinators are routinely flummoxed by these rules. In many cases, frustrated interns spend weeks or even months jumping through the administrative hoops necessary to obtain recognition. Even more damaging from the perspective of successful organizing is that these bureaucratic hassles typically occur at the beginning of the school year—the most important time to recruit students and organize events. Becca, a DM campus coordinator at New York University, spent the period from August until Thanksgiving going back and forth with her school's student activities personnel. Her biggest problem was that the requirements for organizational recognition were not clear. Different administrators gave her conflicting information each time she sought clarification. The irony was that the same office, on a half-dozen occasions, returned the proposed DM constitution Becca had submitted, saying it needed "greater clarity." Furthermore, while the office insisted she revise her official recognition application half-a-dozen times, each of the changes they wanted were, according to Becca, "ridiculous"—both minor and non-substantive. Becca finally gave up and instead met off-campus with the small group of DMers she had been able to recruit. But without official recognition, the chapter was limited in what it could accomplish. By April it no longer existed.

Another example of administrative difficulties occurred at De Anza Community College in California. The officially recognized chapter received notice in November that the club had been suspended. It seems that the faculty member who had agreed to be its advisor was a part-time instructor, and the school had a rule prohibiting such faculty from advising student clubs. The students and the instructor were furious that they had not been informed about the rule, and were being forced to cancel an event they had spent weeks planning. Danielle, the DM intern, was particularly upset that it then took a full month and a half to find a full-time faculty advisor. During that time, members attempted to evade the suspension and continue chapter activities by handing out DM flyers and holding informal meetings in the school's parking lots. But this approach was aborted when they were stopped by De Anza security officers who broke up their meetings and confiscated their flyers.

These were not the only problems that DM chapters encountered. Delays in official recognition frequently occurred when offices failed to respond to requests for recognition in a timely way. At Manhattan College, despite promises from the committee responsible for recognizing student clubs that they would consider DM's application "very soon," the committee kept postponing its meetings and in fact failed to meet with DMers until the very end of the Fall semester. In other cases, even when DM had fulfilled the recognition requirements, the chapter was denied club status. This occurred, for example, when an administrator at Providence College in Rhode Island ruled that the proposed chapter would replicate the work of other clubs on campus—something that, if only it had been true, would have caused us to celebrate. The recognition committee at this school never made explicit which clubs it believed filled that role. In response, Mike, our DM intern, appealed the decision, arguing that there were no other clubs on campus with a mission similar to Democracy Matters. But the application was rejected a second time. Mike was angry that he was never able to learn what exactly had happened—the action seemed completely arbitrary.

At other schools DM interns were warned by students that it was not worth the aggravation of trying to get official recognition. As a result, these interns tried to find other ways to organize on campus and build successful "unofficial" DM chapters. They sometimes secured sponsorship from an academic department, or collaborated with an official school organization such as a political science, sociology, or social justice club. However, in these situations campus coordinators always found such arrangements much too limiting. Invariably, in order to be viable, they had to seek official recognition.

Even official organizational status did not always bring an end to problems with university bureaucracies. DM interns strongly objected to rules that micro-managed what they could do. They confronted onerous regulations concerning trivial issues such as the size and shape of their posters. But more important than such housekeeping regulations was the fact that many schools required prior approval before posters could go up. Not only did this often mean long delays, but more seriously it sometimes involved out-and-out censorship. On more than one occasion approval was denied because the poster's content was deemed to be too "controversial."

Schools frequently also created lengthy, complicated, and restrictive procedures for setting up tables, distributing flyers, showing films, putting notices in student mailboxes, disseminating meeting or event announcements, or chalking on sidewalks. Indeed, it often seemed as if they created rules for every possible idea that a student group might propose. At Indiana University-Purdue University in Indianapolis, a Democracy Matters intern had the idea of organizing an outdoor speak-out with an open microphone, so that students could talk about political issues. Caleb, the DMer, was told that he not only needed to obtain special permission for such an event, but that it could only be held in the University's designated "free speech zone"—a small area that could not begin to accommodate the large crowd Caleb hoped to attract. He explained to his DM field staffer during their weekly phone conversation that the event simply couldn't work in that space. Completely frustrated, he added, "If that's the free speech zone, what does that mean about the rest of the University—no free speech?"

In another instance, when DMers arrived for a scheduled meeting at a room assigned to them by the student activities office, they found that it had been double-booked and another group was already inside. Since it was too late for Amy, the campus coordinator, to reserve a different meeting place, she told attendees to move to another class-room that was open. Soon after the DM meeting started, however, campus security arrived and forced them to leave, on the grounds that the students did not have official permission to use that particular room. Complaints about these kinds of difficulties—some more frustrating or serious than others—were a constant refrain from our student organizers.

In contrast to student activities administrators, university career centers have been helpful in our work. Such offices typically provide students with information about possible internships. Most centers have been willing to include Democracy Matters in their internship postings to students. Numerous DM interns first learned of our program from these offices. Over the years, centers have also assisted us in updating our information and identifying potential interns.

Nevertheless, our overwhelming experience has been that most colleges, rather than making it easy for students to initiate activities, complicate, delay, and sometimes prevent student activism of all kinds. While restrictive rules and the need to acquire official recognition undoubtedly frustrate other student groups as well, this situation presents unique difficulties for Democracy Matters. As a political organization, our requests for official status too often attract intense scrutiny and negative reactions. In addition, compared to other student groups, administrative obstacles and restrictions to chapter activities are more damaging for DMers. What may be a minor inconvenience to other groups is a costly barrier for us because our objective of student political activism is so much more difficult to achieve.

FACULTY

Despite our disappointment with university administrators, we continued to hope that faculty would be a source of support for Democracy Matters. Early on we had identified a number of ways that faculty might provide assistance— serving as advisors to DM chapters, helping students to integrate their internship with their academic work, and participating in and supporting Democracy Matters campus programs. We also wanted to enlist faculty to inform students about the DM internship and to recommend potential interns.

We believed that many of our colleagues would want to see their students involved in Democracy Matters. In a 2001 article about Democracy Matters in the official publication of the American Sociological Association, Kerry Strand agreed. She wrote that faculty involvement in DM would be especially attractive to our own cohort of faculty, "baby-boomers who were involved in direct political action during college [and who] have continued that activism in some form throughout their lives." Strand's article, received by thousands of sociologists throughout the country, explicitly endorsed Democracy Matters as "an organization whose goal is giving college students a meaningful introduction to political involvement."[32] We anticipated that faculty would become active partners with Democracy Matters.

The fact is, however, that over the years very few faculty have involved themselves in DM activism. Our interns reported difficulties even in finding faculty members willing to sign on as advisors. There were cases when this unwillingness actually cost us a chapter—for example, at a school that required an advisor to be secured before official chapter recognition was granted. In declining to help, faculty most often claimed they did not have the time. In response, we instructed campus coordinators to emphasize that only a minimal commitment of time would be required. They would only need to be "paper" advisors because the DM staff would guide the chapter's work. This tactic did result in more faculty signing on as advisors, but a surprising number still refused to help even in this minimal way.

There were of course exceptions—faculty who actively supported and involved themselves in the work of Democracy Matters chapters and helped to mentor DM students on their campuses. One professor at Gettysburg College in Pennsylvania, for example, each year offered his students the chance to organize a Democracy Matters chapter as one of several options in his service-learning class. And an assistant professor of political science at Florida State University in Tallahassee provided constant support to DM students. During her three years as advisor, she attended almost every chapter meeting, helping students to plan and implement campus campaigns and events. An intern at this school commented, "She was so important to us. She got other faculty involved, always encouraged us, and had great ideas about how to build a really strong chapter." Unfortunately, this faculty member was denied tenure and the chapter was never able to replace her with an equally dedicated faculty advisor.

In sum, over the years, only a handful of faculty members have taken much interest in Democracy Matters. No doubt part of the reason for faculty's disengagement lies in the universities' incentive system. Professors are accorded prestige and compensation based on their research and publications. Untenured assistant professors have only a limited number of years to produce the scholarship, participate in enough university service committees, and develop the teaching expertise required to become permanent members of the faculty. The only reward for out-of-classroom involvement with students for faculty members is their own personal gratification.

Furthermore, the pool of faculty to whom students might reasonably look for support is in relative decline. Universities and colleges have increasingly come to rely on part-time and adjunct faculty with short-term appointments. To expect these instructors to interact with students in an intensive way is completely unrealistic. Filling contingent and low-paid positions, these faculty teach multiple classes and often work at more than one job. They simply do not have the time to be closely involved with Democracy Matters chapters.

But even with all this, it still is disturbing that so many faculty—especially the many who believe themselves to be politically liberal, concerned with social issues, and worried about student apathy—take so little interest in their DM students.

STUDENT POLITICAL ENGAGEMENT IN HIGHER EDUCATION

We cannot be definitive about the extent to which Democracy Matters has been harmed by bureaucratic obstacles and faculty indifference. We do not know how important it is that student activities administrators steer students away from political involvement. We have no counter-factual analysis that allows us to estimate how much larger Democracy Matters would be if these impediments were not present. What we do know, however, is that such barriers are ubiquitous. DM students are constantly frustrated by opaque rules and by resistant administrators who prevent their undertaking organizing activities.

These bureaucratic impediments are certainly obstacles to student political engagement. So too is the anti-political bias of national civic engagement organizations and campus volunteer centers. There simply is no way to know how many students would have been attracted to Democracy Matters had we been allowed to compete for their attention with the same level of university endorsement and encouragement that tutoring services, volunteering in soup kitchens, and charity drives receive. Similarly, with respect to faculty, our interns would have clearly benefited if they had met more than a deafening silence from faculty members.

Colleges and universities could and should do better at promoting political involvement and democratic participation. Doing so would not in any way jeopardize a school's commitment to academic freedom or free discourse. The anti-political bias of student activities is unnecessary, and to the extent it affects students, it has a negative effect on the country's democracy. Potential leaders are directed away from politics. The skills required to become effective participants in democratic deliberation are left undeveloped. Furthermore, arbitrary rules and administrative hassles serve no positive function, and act not only to irritate all participants but also to stymie creativity. Students should be allowed wide latitude in exercising initiative to learn about and interact with the world around them. And if increased faculty attentiveness to their students might have some costs in terms of forgone research, it would likely have a payoff pedagogically. The insights faculty would gain about the interests and concerns of their students and the relationships they could build together would enhance both the faculty's teaching and the students' education.

CHAPTER 7

DM STUDENT ACTIVISM

Every year, Democracy Matters chapters produce a profusion of different campaigns, events, and activities. Each campus chapter is free to decide and develop its own approach to organizing. Here, we profile five different DM chapters in order to explore some important political and organizational conundrums that emerge in the course of campus organizing. We also illustrate the wide variety of strategies and tactics that DMers employ. The examples chosen for this overview represent the variety of campuses and situations that typify the DM experience.

BROWN UNIVERSITY

One of our most successful and long-lived Democracy Matters chapters was started in the spring of 2003 at Brown University. Brown, with a little over 6,000 undergraduates, is a prestigious private research university located in Providence, Rhode Island. The school has the reputation of enrolling very bright, politically liberal students, but in 2003 it was not particularly known as a bastion of political activism. For nine consecutive years, it remained one of our largest and most active chapters. It was started by a first-year student, Maya, who had been introduced to Democracy Matters as a high school student when a teacher at the Head Royce School in Berkeley, California, contacted us and asked if he could start a high school DM chapter. Our attempts to interest high school students in working with Democracy Matters have generally borne little fruit. But Maya's school was an exception, and Maya stood out as a leader. Beginning in 2001, Maya, her teacher, and her high school group organized monthly discussions as well as larger assemblies on current political topics. Among the subjects emphasized was the influence of campaign contributions on legislation and social policy.

When Maya informed us in spring 2002 that she would be attending Brown University, we immediately broached the subject of her founding a DM college chapter in the fall. She declined. She was worried about taking on a DM internship during her first year at college when she would not know anyone and everything would be new. She wanted to see what else was going on at Brown. Maya told Joan she was committed to the public funding of campaigns, but she wanted to work for it by joining already established Brown groups rather than by trying to set up an entirely new organization.

Near the end of her first semester, Maya changed her mind. In an early November phone conversation with Joan, she relayed how disappointed she was that, despite a vast array of campus clubs, there was little political activity at Brown. She asked if she could begin a DM internship in the following semester. Even when Joan warned her about the difficulty other interns had in trying to recruit students and start a chapter halfway through the academic year, Maya was undeterred. She had already thought through how she wanted to proceed, and after hearing her plans Joan agreed. From that point on until she graduated four years later, Maya was the driving force behind Brown University's Democracy Matters chapter.

She began by recruiting a core group of Brown students to work with her. She set up a table with Democracy Matters information and a sign-up list at the college's January "activity night," followed up with emails to the students who had signed on, and convinced half a dozen of them to come to an initial meeting. She also contacted students whom she knew were active on campus, and met with each one individually to talk with them about Democracy Matters. Some of these students became part of the initial DM group. In addition, Maya registered Democracy Matters as an official campus chapter, a process that at Brown was relatively uncomplicated.

With this, Maya was ready to schedule a general interest meeting. As a good organizer, she knew that DM's first meeting would be critical for its future success, and she carefully discussed her plans with Beth, the field organizer assigned to Brown. Maya's biggest worry was that she might appear domineering. She had many ideas about what the chapter should do. But she wanted others to share ownership of DM. She and Beth created an agenda that included delegating tasks and forming subcommittees. Students other than Maya would have direct responsibility for publicity, faculty relations, and event planning, while she would help each of them and provide overall coordination. Everyone in the chapter would also be responsible for recruiting new activists. DMers would talk to friends, table, hand out DM flyers in classes, and become Democracy Matters "ambassadors" to other student organizations.

Slowly but surely the chapter grew. From the beginning, Maya and Brown University DMers made a decision—unusual for a Democracy Matters chapter—to focus their attention and organizing not only on the campus, but also in the wider community. At the time, Democracy Matters students at Yale University were also becoming involved with their community. In 2004, they were active participants in the statewide campaign that the following year succeeded in adding Connecticut to the list of states with a public campaign financing option for its legislative seats.

Maya was determined to pass public financing legislation in Rhode Island, and she convinced the others that this should be their long-term goal. She argued that Brown's location would be an asset—Rhode Island was a small state and Providence was the capital city. But to undertake such an ambitious project, she knew that DM at Brown would have to involve not only large numbers of students, but also find allies beyond the university.

By the time students left campus for the summer, the chapter had made great progress. Brown DM boasted twelve committed students, connections to many other campus organizations, and detailed plans for both on- and off-campus organizing in the fall. As Maya wrote in her May end-of-semester report, "We're just getting going—DM here hasn't really been galvanized because of the late start. But just wait until next fall."

Maya was right. Brown's DM chapter prospered. It continued to recruit new members, particularly concentrating on the incoming class of first year students. DMers reached out to campus activists with interesting and well-organized events. They also began to contact state reform organizations to discuss the feasibility of a long-term strategy for passing public campaign financing for state legislative candidates.

Over the next few years, Brown's Democracy Matters students became more experienced and skilled, and therefore even more effective organizers. Beginning in the spring of 2004, for example, they took advantage of the increased political interest and activity associated with the congressional election years. They joined a large coalition of campus groups that were registering students. In their registration work they incorporated a DM message about the damaging role of money in politics and the need for student activism to correct the problem. Working with the coalition not only increased Democracy Matters' visibility, but also developed strong working relationships and trust with activist students. But at the same time, election fever was a two-edged sword. As Maya outlined in her December 2004 report, "It was tough getting students to focus on a non-partisan message like ours when they were so intent on getting [President] Bush out of office. No one was really in the mood to hear about how money in politics affected the Democrats too, because so many students were supporting the Democratic candidate. And when he lost, lots of students became disgusted with politics altogether."

As a way to regain momentum after the election, Brown DM created a series of campus actions to appeal primarily to students disaffected from partisan politics. One approach they adopted was to provide an opportunity for students to vent about the political system. Their anticipation was that if students were able to articulate their frustrations, DMers could be convincing that the source of their disaffection was rooted in how electoral campaigns were funded. Immediately after the election, the chapter created a "Democracy Wall" in the center of the school's main quad. On a huge sheet of paper, students were encouraged to write their thoughts—and criticisms— about the election and the future of American politics. The "Wall" quickly became a location where students actively engaged in political discussion and debate. While DMers staffing the "Wall" emphasized the importance of public campaign financing as critical to a fair democracy, other topics and issues were fervently debated as well.

The chapter also made use of the school paper to re-interest students in political issues. For example, Maya published a long op-ed whose title, "My Uzi Costs a Ton," was purposefully misleading, suggesting that the article had nothing to do with politics. But the op-ed cleverly linked the expiration of a decade-long ban on assault weapons to campaign contributions. Describing how "special interests corrupt our democracy" through "an electoral system that systematically privileges the interests of the well-heeled and well-connected over that of the public good," she concluded that "the influence of money in politics has always posed the greatest threat to the principle of democracy."

Over and beyond these activities, the chapter reprised its "ambassador" strategy. DMers attended the general meetings of a wide variety of campus organizations, talking about Democracy Matters generally, but also explicitly asking groups to endorse and join the fight for statewide public financing. Brown DM ended the semester by throwing a "Reclaiming Your Idealism" party. Co-sponsored by the university's Green Party and the school's Environmental House, it was, as Maya later wrote, a "fun event with a live band and an open mic—a celebratory forum for people to meet and share ideas." At the party they handed out fake $5 bills with a picture of "Mr. Clean" and information about "clean"—publicly financed—campaigns. A highlight of the evening occurred when students dressed as "Democracy Matters Superheroes" staged a fistfight with others dressed as "Fat Cat Politicians."

With all of this, Democracy Matters became a more visible presence on campus, and increasing numbers of Brown students came to see the importance of DM's campaign to reduce the distorting influence of wealth in elections. The chapter had shown that issues students cared about—the environment, gun control, frustration at President Bush's reelection—were all connected to the issue of private money in politics. In this way they convinced many more Brown students to join DM.

During the following years, as Brown DM continued to build on campus, the chapter also worked to gain off-campus allies. DMers were able to create a relationship with the state's Common Cause chapter, and forged ties as well with statewide organizations such as the Sierra Club, the Gray Panthers, the Environmental Council, and Operation Clean Government. In the course of this outreach, Maya learned of a new state-based political coalition, Right Now, that was attempting to pass legislation related to the separation of powers. Even though the coalition's agenda was not directly related to campaign finance reform, Democracy Matters students began attending Right Now meetings, and soon thereafter the chapter joined the coalition. DMers believed that Right Now's goal would strengthen democracy in the state. But even more important, they hoped that the chapter's active participation in the coalition would encourage Right Now organizations to support Democracy Matters' own public financing efforts. As they leafleted and canvassed for the separation of powers, they began to build support for public campaign financing.

As Brown DM students continued their off-campus work, they were often asked by legislators and community members about the specifics of the legislation they were advocating. Some potential supporters refused to endorse a public campaign financing effort until they could review the details of a bill. The problem was that there was no such bill. The DM staff, in discussion with Maya, suggested that the chapter write its own legislation. This idea was novel for the organization and exciting to the students. But neither the staff nor the students knew how to write such legislation. Joan suggested that Maya contact the Brennan Center for Justice, an organization at New York University's Law School that had been instrumental in crafting several state public financing bills. After several conversations with Brennan Center lawyers, Brown DM students invested what Maya described as "hours and hours and hours" on "a major research project." What they had to do was provide Brennan with data on state election spending patterns. With this is hand, and working closely with Brennan lawyers, the Brown chapter helped to draft a public campaign financing bill tailored to the state. With a concrete proposal in hand, they then set about the herculean task of passing their bill.

That December, Maya's end-of-semester report provided an indication of the chapter's legislative ambitions. The report included a list of goals for the following semester: "Have a clean elections bill introduced in the legislature; hold a press conference to gain media attention; research the existing Maine and Arizona public financing systems; involve more professors; develop a state-specific public financing website, flyers and other materials; increase campus DM membership and get more endorsements from student groups."

As their work to achieve public campaign financing continued, the chapter initiated what would become a signature activity of Brown Democracy Matters—testifying at town, county, and state legislative meetings and hearings. Maya wrote of the excitement of their first experience giving testimony to state legislators. She reported that at the separate hearings held by the House Finance Committee and the Senate Judiciary Committee, "In addition to the students who were testifying, we also had an average of fourteen students attending with signs and silk-screened T-shirts with our clean elections logo. It was thrilling."

Following the hearings, a member of Brown Democracy Matters reported on the work of its members in the school paper. Its efforts were also featured in a mainstream city newspaper and as a front-page article of Providence's alternative paper. Chapter members were also interviewed by the campus radio station and by several in the city. All of this was extremely gratifying, but it took, according to Maya, "an ungodly number of meetings of committees, subcommittees, and individual contact outreach meetings!"

All of this work gave the chapter momentum. A diverse group of campus organizations including Students for Sensible Drug Policy, the Asian-American Association, the Chinese Students' Association, Model UN, the Queer Alliance, and the Feminist Majority endorsed DM's public financing bill. Off campus, the League of Women Voters, Catholic Pastoral Council, Service Employees International Union, and American Association of Retired People agreed to work with DM's growing coalition. Maya's and other DMers' commitment to this political work was so strong that they did not want the university's summer vacation to interrupt their organizing. She and four others decided to spend the summer in Providence so they could continue to work in the community. As she reflected in her May report on what was a truly amazing year, Maya concluded: "It's been great to see how far we've come this year, but it's kind of intimidating to feel at times as if us Democracy Matters kids are the ones single-handedly trying to push this incredibly difficult reform along—but exciting too!"

Over the years, the Brown Democracy Matters chapter continued to grow and develop both its organizing capacity and political sophistication. What is especially remarkable was its stability in the face of the inevitable turnover in student membership that occurred annually. Seniors graduate and a new cohort of students arrives each year. At most schools, Democracy Matters interns change as well. Though some chapters have managed it, it is extremely difficult to keep up the momentum year after year. In the case of Brown, however, the fact that Maya remained a DM intern for three and a half years was very important to maintaining continuity. But equally important were her charisma and talent. She pushed the chapter to continue petition and letter-writing campaigns, publishing articles in the school paper and printing its own newsletters. Most importantly, Maya made sure that Brown Democracy Matters placed a high priority on recruiting and carefully training new members. As a result, the chapter was able to build on its earlier successes and remain strong long after Maya had graduated.

Maya finished her undergraduate coursework in December 2006. She told us she wanted to stay at Brown until the summer so that she could continue to work with Democracy Matters. Eager to retain her organizing talent as long as possible, we offered Maya a five-month part-time Democracy Matters staff position. Her job would be twofold: she would work to organize DM chapters in high schools and at other colleges and universities in the state; and she would help the Brown chapter in its transition to life without Maya. As it happened, the results of that spring effort were not exactly what we or Maya had anticipated.

Assigning Maya to work with high schools reflected our hope that we could build chapters at secondary schools. Earlier we had created Democracy Matters High School Fellowships that we thought would attract interest. Compared to our college interns, our high school DMers would be asked to commit much less time to Democracy Matters, and would not be paid a stipend. They would receive Democracy Matters materials and mentoring, and be invited to the DM Summits. In this way, we thought we had crafted an attractive approach; one that made limited demands but that nonetheless would expose high schoolers to the world of political money and political organizing. We expected that many of these students would later want to become interns and DM activists when they enrolled at a college or university. Early on, we were optimistic about the potential for expanding Democracy Matters chapters in this way. But our high school program had never really taken off. Over the years, we had only a few successful chapters. We hoped that given Maya's experience as a Democracy Matters high school leader, she would be able to craft a more successful strategy for high school students.

In addition, we hoped Maya would be able to increase the number of DM college chapters in the state. In the past, many DM interns had expressed the desire to involve their friends at other schools around the country. Even when they did not know anyone at nearby schools, they were eager to try to establish DM clubs with which they could collaborate. Yet none of these efforts had borne fruit. We felt that Maya's statewide contacts and obvious organizing ability would serve as a good test of whether either of these strategies for expanding Democracy Matters was viable.

After a full semester of trying however, it was all too clear that Maya's efforts had failed. Though she worked hard, she was not able to add a single high school or college Democracy Matters chapter to our list. Extremely frustrated by the experience, Maya told us that she had no explanation for why college students on other campuses had not responded to her urging that they start Democracy Matters chapters. With respect to her inability to recruit high school students however, she explained that a major obstacle was the rejection by high school administrators of any clubs or organizations that seemed political. In addition, she reported, most high school students with whom she talked simply did not have enough information about or interest in current affairs or the political system to see money in politics as important to them. We continue to offer high school fellowships and to encourage our interns to reach out to other campuses. But in light of Maya's experience, we have come to recognize that neither approach is likely to result in a significant expansion in the number of DM chapters.

The outcome of the second aspect of her job that spring—working with Brown DMers—was also unanticipated. In April, with Maya's encouragement, Brown DMers came to us with suggestions for a new organizational structure for their chapter. First, they wanted to rotate chapter leadership among a small executive board. The DM intern would change each semester. Second, Brown would no longer consult with Democracy Matters staff concerning the selection of interns. Instead, the intern would be chosen exclusively by a chapter election.

These proposals created a dilemma for us. Although we wanted to respect the students' plans, we had serious reservations. We were concerned that rotating internships would weaken the chapter. We also wondered whether elections would result in the selecting of the best organizers. Might the election only turn into a popularity contest that would not serve the interests of Democracy Matters? Further, we did not understand why the students were rejecting our mentoring role. After all, we had worked successfully with Maya and Brown DM since its inception, and frankly were reluctant to change an approach that had proved effective. Yet, in a sense, this was exactly what we had hoped for—Democracy Matters students becoming independent political activists, willing to experiment with new ways of carrying out their work. Given the strength of the chapter and our confidence in Maya's endorsement of these proposals, we decided to encourage Brown's experimentation and see where the new model took us.

It turned out, however, that the implementation of these changes weakened the chapter. With interns turning over each semester, there was less time for the DM staff to train and build strong ties with them. The chapter's interns rarely solicited the DM staff's advice. Though they did adhere to the mandatory weekly phone call with staff, it was often difficult for the field organizer to obtain clear insight into the chapter's functioning. Several of the campus coordinators who followed Maya were weak, students with poorly developed leadership and organizing skills to whom Joan would never have extended internship offers. The chapter no longer used Democracy Matters materials, preferring instead to create its own. Campus visits by Democracy Matters' staff were eagerly sought by other chapters—we always had many more requests than we could accommodate. But Brown DM extended no such invitations. And though many Brown DMers attended the annual DM Summits, the gap between the chapter and the national organization grew.

As part of the process of disengagement, Brown Democracy Matters also changed its political agenda. After many years of trying, they gave up the effort to secure public financing in the state. Though its statewide work continued, the group drifted to a less radical politics, emphasizing disclosure of campaign contributions and promoting general political dialogue and engagement among students. We were also disappointed that a 2011 political "boot camp" for college students organized by the chapter offered not a single workshop on money in politics, despite the fact that our staff had offered to facilitate one. If the Summit's discussion of the Iraq War was a test of whether DMers could engage in reasoned discourse when they disagreed, our relationship with Brown Democracy Matters was a test of another kind. How much programmatic diversity would we tolerate?

To watch the chapter drift away from concentration on public financing raised the question of whether our subsidizing the Brown group was still justified. We were, after all, an organization with a specific political message. While it was perfectly within its rights for the Brown group to shape its own viewpoint, it was by the same token reasonable for us to consider whether the chapter still articulated the Democracy Matters' political perspective. To the extent that the latter was not true, a good argument could be made to no longer offer the club DM internships.

Ultimately, we decided not to follow the cancellation route. Despite the fact that relations grew frosty, we continued to support Brown DM. Two considerations were paramount in this decision. The first was that though campaign finance reform had been assigned a lower priority than we would have preferred, Brown DM did not drop it altogether. It remained among its goals. We really could not make the argument that a total political rupture had occurred.

But the more important argument was that the very separation we so regretted could be interpreted as a success. What had happened is that we had nurtured the growth of a campus group that not only had sustained itself over many years—an all too rare occurrence—but that as well had developed a capacity for autonomous thinking. It turned out that in doing so the group moved away from us politically. But in the larger sense it was hard not to recognize this as an organizing triumph. In the first place, Brown DM had sustained political activism at a level that matched or exceeded the experience of almost all other chapters. In the second place, it still was in a general sense on our side politically, though not in the way that we would have wished. In the end, therefore, we overcame our hesitation and did what political coalition-building calls for. We emphasized our agreements and, without denying the reality of differences, continued to support Brown University Democracy Matters.

SUNY NEW PALTZ

The New York State University at New Paltz has a very different culture than Brown's. It is a medium-size public state university, located in a small town rather than a city, and is much less selective in its admissions policy than is Brown. New Paltz has a solid but not outstanding academic reputation, and is known to attract counter-cultural young people who might have been labeled hippies in an earlier era. The campus has a large number of student groups focused on the environment, alternative lifestyle issues, and identity politics. There is more political awareness at New Paltz than on most cam-puses, but campus activism tends to take the form of sporadic protests and lifestyle choices rather than a sustained effort to have an impact on legislation and the political system.

The Democracy Matters chapter at New Paltz made use of many of the tactics of outreach and education that were used at Brown—tabling, writing op-eds, giving short "raps" in classes, as well as peti-tion and educational poster campaigns. In addition, the New Paltz chapter implemented several other creative campaigns, culminating in a very large special event near the end of the year.

Nate, the intern who founded the chapter at New Paltz in 2005, had previously worked as a DM intern at the nearby Ulster County Community College. This was one of the few community colleges where Democracy Matters was able to establish itself. Such schools are famously difficult to organize. Community college students usu-ally do not live on campus and attend for only one or two years. Many of them are adults with full-time jobs and families who come to cam-pus only when their classes are scheduled. Under these circumstances, community colleges rarely can boast a vibrant campus life with strong organizations and clubs. Nate was a talented and dedicated organizer. But though he worked hard for two years, ultimately Ulster County Community College Democracy Matters gained only limited traction on campus. After Nate transferred to New Paltz, the chapter dissolved.

In contrast to the barren nature of campus life experienced at Ulster County Community College, what Nate found at New Paltz in the fall of 2005 was exhilarating. In this countercultural mecca, all kinds of groups, causes, and activities competed for attention. To attract support for Democracy Matters, Nate thought he needed to make what he called "a big splash." For such an event to be a success, he believed that it would have to be preceded by a year of active organizing that could draw in large numbers from both the campus and the community.

After recruiting a core group of DM activists to work with him, and obtaining official campus status, the chapter applied for and secured a budget of several thousand dollars to support a spring event that it called "Money in Politics: The Root of All Evil." Nate's idea was to fill a room that held over five hundred people for a panel discussion addressing several issues at the same time—all tied to election financing.

The DM group at New Paltz put on successful "Root of All Evil" events for three consecutive years. Each was long—typically lasting more than four hours—with a panel composed of students, faculty, and local activists. Each speaker offered a short presentation outlining a different critical social issue or problem. Depending on the year, these included a long list of topics—the war in Iraq, rising college tuition, poverty, sexism, right-wing media, gay rights, health care, global warming, civil rights, and the de-criminalization of marijuana. Joan represented Democracy Matters, and after each speaker, she briefly explained how the problem just discussed was linked to big campaign contributions and how a system of public financing of elections was necessary.

Nate and his chapter members did a great job of building interest in the event, advertising it throughout the year both on and off campus, and attracting media attention and group co-sponsorships. Describing their strategy of working with other groups, Nate explained, "We wanted to make Democracy Matters a part of other organizations' events. If we really help them they will be there for us for the 'Root.'" Each year New Paltz DMers worked closely with groups on voter registration and get-out-the vote campaigns, especially the large, state-funded Public Interest Research Group on campus. Together they convinced the university not only to make available voter registration forms during first-year orientation, but also to offer a form to every student who made a purchase at the university bookstore. During the year, the DM chapter co-sponsored other events as well—a Rock Against Racism concert, a Mother Earth Day, a rally protesting the war in Iraq, and a Rosa Parks Poetry Slam.

Nate's personal creativity made Democracy Matters events especially effective. Around Halloween, for example, he designed a "Haunted House of Democracy" maze that DMers constructed on campus. As New Paltz students traveled through the maze they were confronted with graphic illustrations of the horrors of war, hunger, child poverty, racism, and the lack of health care. But when they reached the end of the maze, they entered the "Democracy Matters Room" lined with displays and information about how getting big private money out of politics with public campaign financing would help overcome the "horrors." Later in the year, Nate built giant puppets and used them to stage improv skits on campus depicting a "DM public financing crusader" doing battle with a "fat cat politician."

Nate himself became an increasingly passionate advocate of full public campaign financing. During his last year at New Paltz, he developed the idea of creating a statewide voting bloc of people pledged to vote only for candidates who supported full public campaign financing. Nate felt so strongly about this innovation that he decided to form a new organization that would focus exclusively on getting voters to sign such a pledge. As earlier with Brown University, we were faced with a dilemma when Nate asked us if he could work on building his organization as a DM intern. He wanted to fold his Democracy Matters internship into work with his new organization. What gave us pause was that his efforts would almost entirely be directed at non-students. But at the same time, we wanted to encourage Nate's political development. It took some doing, but we finally came to an understanding that Nate's internship for the rest of the year would include work on both his pledge idea and his regular campus-based organizing.

The arrangement worked well. And even now, many years after his graduation, Nate continues to gather still more voter pledges in support of public campaign financing.

Though Nate and the New Paltz chapter accomplished a great deal, there was a downside as well. In the two years he was our intern, Nate never was able to recruit a significant number of core members who stuck with the chapter over time. But what surprised us was how much New Paltz DM actually accomplished with a small membership. According to Paula, Nate's DM field organizer, the chapter's success was primarily the result of Nate's own unflagging commitment. Nate literally ate, slept, and breathed public financing. At the same time, perhaps because of his passion, he lacked the patience to carefully train less experienced and committed students. Indeed, Nate's seriousness and single-minded devotion made it difficult for him to understand and connect to typical New Paltz students and even to some DMers. Though he and Paula often discussed the problem, and Nate tried to adopt many of her suggestions for recruiting and delegating, he was such a perfectionist that he frequently ended up trying to do everything by himself. The consequence was that when he graduated, Nate did not leave behind a cohort of younger students dedicated to the organization who could carry on New Paltz DM in his footsteps.

The chapter did survive for a year after Nate left, but with considerably less success. Nate had suggested that Frida, a junior majoring in history, apply for the internship. Joan was dubious, but deferred to Nate's judgment that Frida would do a good job. However despite our support, she was unable to sustain a viable chapter at New Paltz. She started out the year well enough—largely building on Nate's legacy—but the momentum did not last for more than a couple of months. While she regularly reported to Paula that the chapter was working on another "Root of All Evil," in the end the event never came off. Nate's creativity and passion were not replaced. Without a strong campus coordinator able to reverse the downhill slide, there was little remaining of a Democracy Matters chapter at the university by the end of the year.

Our experience at New Paltz was reflected on a number of DM campuses over the years. Effective interns would succeed in building dynamic chapters capable of mobilizing the campus, but subsequent campus coordinators often were unable to sustain those efforts. Sometimes only weak intern candidates were available to head up the chapter. In these cases we frequently offered internships to individuals we might not otherwise have chosen to be campus coordinators. Our hope was that, given its strength in the past, if we could sustain the chapter—even at a lower level of activity than previously—a stronger leader might emerge from within it. Happily for us, this did sometimes occur. But more often, weak intern campus coordinators produced weak results, with no prospective new leadership emerging.

Sometimes the problem was that the intern who followed a particularly talented predecessor tried to replicate what the previous intern had done, rather than creating his or her own organizing style. In other cases, the new intern had badly underestimated the effort required to nurture a successful Democracy Matters chapter. Jen, a campus coordinator who found herself in that situation, wrote in her end of the semester report, "I never thought it would be so hard. Last year things went great and I guess I didn't realize how hard Pete [the earlier intern] had to work at this."

What we learned is that in the end it is the performance of the intern that is most responsible for the success or failure of a Democracy Matters chapter. With a dedicated and capable intern like Nate, Democracy Matters at New Paltz had a profound impact on both the campus and wider community. But with the loss of that talent, a once vibrant chapter became less effective, and eventually collapsed. Its resurgence would have to await another strong leader.

BLOOMSBURG UNIVERSITY

Bloomsburg University was another campus that, somewhat like New Paltz, created a signature Democracy Matters event. The annual "All-Day Dialogue" was the brainchild of our first intern there, Jeff, who in 2003 founded a chapter and established an active core of Democracy Matters students.

Bloomsburg, with an undergraduate student body roughly the size of Brown's, is located near the small town of the same name in Pennsylvania. The campus, like so many others across the country, boasts a large number of student clubs as well as a fraternity and sorority system.

The Bloomsburg chapter remained strong for a number of years, with three other effective campus coordinators following Jeff. DM at Bloomsburg constructed its own website, spoke in local high school classes, and organized lobbying excursions to talk with state legislators about public campaign financing. Its many activities were regularly featured in the school's newspaper and occasionally even by the local press. From the beginning, Jeff and Democracy Matters at Bloomsburg worked hard to build coalitions with campus groups including the College Democrats, College Republicans, the Pan-Hellenic and Inter-Fraternity Councils, the Student-Town Unification Coalition, and the student government.

Unusual for many campuses, Bloomsburg DMers received strong support from the school's administration. The president of Bloomsburg University, for example, invited the chapter to participate in its Freshman Orientation Week. Each year a DM staff member addressed the entire class of incoming first-year students during that week. Bloomsburg administrators also enlisted DM in organizing the administration-supported voter registration drive on campus. Democracy Matters students were also featured speakers during the annual campus celebration of Constitution Day in mid-September—a major event at Bloomsburg.

Faculty at Bloomsburg too were supportive of Democracy Matters. For example, during the voter registration drive, a professor of political science, Jim Waldman, approached the chapter with the idea of producing a satirical video with them about student political apathy and the importance of registering to vote. Chapter members created the video and circulated it on campus, inviting everyone to see Professor Waldman "starring" in his first theatrical role.

In some ways, however, the support for Democracy Matters by the university's administrators, faculty, and student organizations was costly. Jeff especially worried that it diluted the Democracy Matters message. He was concerned that the university was co-opting the DM chapter. For example when Bloomsburg's president invited DM to speak at Freshman Orientation, she made it clear that we were being asked to briefly introduce Democracy Matters, but to confine most of our remarks to the importance of registering to vote and going to the polls. She clearly implied, without quite saying it, that DM should avoid presenting its analysis of how private wealth distorts the political process.

The hours spent registering students to vote, filming the satirical video, and preparing for Constitution Day left little time for DMers to spread their own message about money and politics. Despite his worry about being co-opted, in these cases Jeff saw these activities as valuable, especially for initially establishing a Democracy Matters presence on campus. The speaking opportunity during Freshman Orientation informed every incoming student about DM and afforded legitimacy to the organization. Speaking at Constitution Day provided even more visibility. Jeff also believed that working with the student government on voting and voter registration was important for the chapter. His end-of-semester report concluded, "I'd be lying if I didn't say that more than half our school knows about and likes Democracy Matters."

But neither Bloomsburg DMers nor Jeff was satisfied with the chapter's neglecting its critical edge by confining itself to registering students to vote or celebrating the Constitution as a symbol of democracy. To break out of this confinement, Jeff came up with the idea of an "All-Day Dialogue." With this, Democracy Matters could choose its own message and shape the content of the event. The first All-Day Dialogue, as well as subsequent ones, occurred at a large central campus location. The room in which it was held was encircled with booths and tables displaying materials about Democracy Matters and other campus organizations co-sponsoring the event. Someone from the Democracy Matters Speaker's Bureau stood in the center of the room, with chairs positioned in a semicircle. During each successive class period, faculty members brought their students to participate in the "dialogue," creating an audience of hundreds of students by the end of the day.

Joan represented Democracy Matters that first year. Though Jeff had explained generally what to expect, she was stunned by the actual event. She ended up talking for almost seven hours to over a dozen classes in sociology, economics, political science, history, and biology. As each class arrived, the faculty member briefly outlined what they had been discussing recently. Joan then tied the class subject to money in politics. Most links were obvious. She talked with an introductory biology class about the health care industry's efforts to use campaign contributions to block health care reform. With an American history class, she focused on the connection between war and the political power of wealthy corporations producing military equipment. Another topic concerned global climate change and the role oil companies play in the continuing United States dependence on fossil fuels. The DMers were excited that their idea for a dialogue had actually worked, and Joan was exhausted but exhilarated.

After Jeff graduated, the Bloomsburg Democracy Matters chapter was led by a series of other strong interns. They retained his emphasis on nurturing good relationships with students, faculty, and the administration, but they also developed their own initiatives. For example, Bloomsburg DM decided to get involved at the state level by trying to move public financing legislation. However, the DM chapter was never able to achieve the traction on this issue that Brown had. Bloomsburg was located in a much larger state with a more complicated political landscape and a conservative legislature. Furthermore, though they tried, Bloomsburg students could not convince the many citizen organizations active in the state to work with them.

Nonetheless, the Bloomsburg students did make some progress in their legislative efforts. They identified and met with a state legislator willing to explore introducing a judicial public campaign financing bill. Two states—North Carolina and New Mexico—already had laws that offered the option of public campaign funding to candidates for judicial races. Bloomsburg DMers had studied those experiences, and believed that a proposal for a judicial option might work in their state. On campus, they passed out information and held discussions about judicial public financing and organized several trips to the state capitol to lobby their legislators. Dana, the 2008 DM intern, summed up their efforts in her report: "Aside from our all-day dialogue and a great Earth Day celebration co-sponsored with lots of other campus groups, our main focus this year was to create awareness about judicial public financing. It didn't work so well with the legislators, but students on campus really got behind the idea."

Dana led the chapter for two consecutive years. The way in which Dana became involved with Democracy Matters is instructive, illustrating as it does how serendipitous the process of becoming a political activist often is. In her internship interview with Joan, Dana explained that she had arrived as a first-year student at Bloomsburg knowing exactly what she wanted to do with her life. She was ready to declare a major in marine biology and prepare for a career as a scientific researcher. She had no interest in politics at all. At the school's student activities night, she signed up for all kinds of campus clubs, but ended up not joining any of them. Their meetings were boring, she said, and she was busy with labs and classes.

But one of Dana's classes that first semester was on the media. She took it, she said, only because it fit her schedule, fulfilled a requirement, and "didn't meet at 8:30 a.m." Though Dana was not especially taken with the subject matter, she liked the professor and enjoyed the outside speakers he brought in. One day in the middle of the semester, a "very cool" guest speaker announced to the class that the following day she would be participating on campus in something called an "all-day dialogue." Dana's professor said he would be attending too, and urged the students to join him. Dana did not plan on going. In fact, as she told Joan, she had totally forgotten about it. But when she happened to be walking by and saw the speaker and her professor, she stopped. She ended up staying for the rest of the day. Two days later, Dana went to the Democracy Matters regular weekly meeting, even though she said she was "totally intimidated" because she knew nothing about politics. But by April she had learned. Dana became the DM intern for the next two years. She was a terrific leader, and after graduation she went on to a career in political organizing.

There are many stories like Dana's—though perhaps none quite so dramatic—that reinforce our conviction that there are students everywhere who, if exposed to our political ideas and actions would, like Dana, get hooked. Unfortunately, the Bloomsburg DM chapter fell apart after she graduated. We offered an internship to a student recommended by the chapter, but soon enough we were forced to withdraw it. After the first month of school, the new intern began to miss her weekly calls with the staff, and Dana—who had remained in touch with Democracy Matters students at Bloomsburg—contacted us to report that meetings were being cancelled and little was being accomplished. Dana was able to find another chapter member to take over the internship, but the student who came forward—though making a valiant effort for several months—was unable to revitalize the chapter. So after that year, to Dana's dismay and our disappointment, Bloomsburg University no longer had a Democracy Matters chapter.

ST. LAWRENCE UNIVERSITY

Democracy Matters at St. Lawrence University, a small liberal arts college in rural, upstate New York had a interrupted history. Initially, DM had a successful two year run, but then it collapsed, only to be reborn three years later. Though the initial chapter was short-lived, during those years its core of students was extremely active. In addition to general campus outreach and education on public financing, their organizing had a specific focus that arose from their dissatisfaction with an aspect of life on their own campus. St. Lawrence DM members were upset that elections for their college student government were dominated by candidates who could afford to purchase expensive posters, giveaways, and other promotions. They were incensed that, not just in national politics but even so close to home, money unfairly skewed elections in favor of relatively wealthy candidates.

DM at St. Lawrence decided to try to reform their campus election process by instituting a college form of "public financing." By making an issue of the unfairness of their own campus elections, they thought they could both correct an injustice at the school and at the same time illustrate—in an immediate way—the desirability of public campaign financing in state and national politics.

The issue of money dominating student government elections had previously come up on other DM campuses, and several chapters had tried to change their school's rules. After a campaign at Wesleyan University in Connecticut, for example, DMers were able to convince their student council to put limits on the amount of money student candidates could spend. But the council disagreed with the chapter's real goal—to provide financial support, that is "public financing," for all qualified student candidates. In the other cases, efforts to change the school's election systems met with early failure.

But at St. Lawrence in 2007, DMers actually succeeded in passing and implementing a system of public financing. Their "Clean and Fair Elections" system gave student candidates, who chose to "run clean," a set amount with which to fund their campaigns. Sam, St. Lawrence's DM intern, conveyed in his end-of-semester report the chapter's excitement when the new system was installed: "Our first 'clean election' was wildly successful. Eight of the nine candidates for the student government executive board ran clean, and everyone elected was a clean candidate. They told us that they could not have won without the money provided by student government. The publicity was great for educating the campus about Democracy Matters and about campaign finance reform."

Sam also described how hard DMers had to work in order to win "public financing." They wrote op-eds in the school paper, held informational meetings in dorms, made class announcements, and spoke to campus clubs. They also used posters, flyers, and other publicity to get student opinion behind them. According to Sam, most stressful were the hours spent meeting, lobbying, and presenting arguments to student council members.

Unfortunately, after two successful years, the St. Lawrence chapter dissolved. We were unable to find an intern who had the necessary time and leadership ability required by a Democracy Matters chapter. Joan did interview two chapter members who expressed interest in following Sam as an intern. They were both well qualified to lead DM. During the interview however, one of the students expressed concern about the amount of work it would take to sustain the chapter. Soon afterward, she emailed Joan saying that she was sorry but she would not have the time necessary to do a good job. The other student, Barra, accepted the internship even though she had worried during the interview about living up to the standards set by previous interns. As it turned out, only two weeks into the semester, Barra resigned in tears, leaving St. Lawrence without an intern and without a Democracy Matters chapter.

St. Lawrence's "clean and fair" elections lasted for another year. But in the following year, without a strong Democracy Matters to defend it, the system was repealed by the student government. We continued to send our internship information to St. Lawrence's career-planning office, student activities center, and faculty with requests to inform their students of the opportunity. But we heard nothing from the school. Then, three years later, Joan received an email from Hossein, a St. Lawrence student she had never met. He explained that he and few other students were engaged in a project for a political science class that involved organizing a Democracy Matters chapter. He invited Joan to speak at the school and said he wanted to apply for an internship for the following year.

Excited about the prospects of revitalizing the St. Lawrence chapter, but not knowing what to expect, Joan drove to the school. She was both surprised and gratified to find that the students had prepared a full day of activities for her on campus. Typically, when a DM staff member makes a campus visit, the chapter is asked to arrange a series of events: a large all-campus discussion or lecture; a newspaper interview; a meeting with chapter members; and guest lectures in classes or meetings with faculty and administrators. But because this was not an ordinary situation, Joan had not made any such requests of the St. Lawrence students. Without any prompting, however, they had organized all the elements of a typical DM campus visit. That evening when Joan sat down to interview Hossein and Shellie, a student with whom Hossein wanted to share the internship, she was ready to hire them both. Her only hesitation was whether they would work well together or whether, as had been the case on several other DM campuses, having two interns at the same time would reduce their effectiveness. But they made a strong argument that their skills were complementary: Shellie was outgoing and charismatic with natural leadership ability; and Hossein was passionate about public financing and loved to think about strategy and tactics. Together with others, they had already developed plans for the chapter, though they made it clear that they were not interested in revisiting the issue of on-campus student elections. So despite an interruption, Democracy Matters again was organizing student activists at St. Lawrence.

CALVIN COLLEGE

Right from the beginning, we encountered disagreement with Democracy Matters students at Calvin College, a private, religiously affiliated college in Grand Rapids, Michigan. The problem centered on DM's core political commitment. The students in the chapter at Calvin were interested in politics all right, but not really in campaign finance reform.

During the one year we had a chapter at Calvin, DM students comprised a large, active, and successful group, eager to encourage political debates and discussion on their campus. The chapter also initiated several effective action projects. But all of these events were limited to voter registration campaigns and efforts to get-out-the-vote on Election Day 2008. Throughout the entire year, the chapter's members resisted the pressure from Alan, their DM field organizer, to focus on the issue of money and politics. Nevertheless, we were reluctant to cut off the internship at Calvin. This especially was the case because our intern, Stacy, continually assured us that the members would soon follow our suggestions. We kept thinking that they would eventually get it.

We had been particularly enthusiastic about the prospect of establishing a Democracy Matters chapter at a place like Calvin College. It had a reputation as being conservative, and for us that was a plus. We did not want DM to be confined to liberal campuses. We thought it was important to bring our organizing to schools where progressive thinking was all but absent. In addition, Stacy seemed to have great potential as an organizer. Her application and her interview, like so many of those who applied to Democracy Matters, revealed an energetic, charismatic student who had experience in leadership positions in several campus groups. Furthermore, during the previous year Stacy had worked in the university's volunteer office, helping to increase student involvement in the local community. During her interview, she expressed interest in moving in a more political direction. She felt that solving many of the problems Calvin's student volunteers were addressing could only be fixed through political engagement. This of course was music to our ears. The fact that Stacy herself seemed politically naïve, that she had not thought much about money in politics or even heard of public campaign financing was not that unusual among DM applicants. She seemed eager, well organized, and motivated. She could learn what she had to. Stacy was the kind of student with whom Democracy Matters often had great success.

The Fall semester started off very well. In September, Alan traveled to the campus to meet with Stacy and several students she had already recruited as DM members. He spent an afternoon talking with them about organizing and campaign finance reform, and helping them plan the semester's projects. Alan came back excited about

Calvin students' enthusiasm and creative ideas, and with their potential to develop an outstanding chapter.

Because it was a presidential election year and DM's first year at Calvin, Stacy wanted to introduce Democracy Matters to the campus by organizing a voter-registration campaign. She thought it would be a good way to have Democracy Matters become known on campus, and to show that we were non-partisan and committed to an inclusive democracy. Talking with Alan, chapter members outlined an ambitious strategy. They wanted to create a coalition with Calvin Republicans, Libertarians, and Democrats to staff weekly tables registering students to vote. They also planned to make presentations in classes and dorms, and create pamphlets with information about the candidates. Their idea was to contact professors and dorm counselors to set up programs in residence halls. They also wanted to implement a campus-wide publicity campaign until Election Day, urging students to register and vote. For late October, they planned a big party they called "Amps Against Apathy—You Can Vote." With music provided by popular student and local bands and with speakers emphasizing the importance of the student vote, they thought they could draw a large crowd. The "price" of admission would be proof of registration or the willingness to register on the spot.

Calvin DMers spent most of September and October implementing their plan. By Election Day they had accomplished everything they set out to do. During this time, Alan was so impressed with the chapter's growth and activism that he decided not to push the students to include information on money in politics as part of their organizing. But after the voter-registration deadline had passed, he told them it was time to focus on public financing. He urged them to create an event that illustrated the harmful role of money in the upcoming election. But that was not what the students wanted to do. Instead, the Calvin DMers wanted to work on getting students to vote on Election Day. In explanation, Stacy told Alan, "It really doesn't do any good to register so many people if they don't actually end up voting." So with their usual energy, Calvin DMers set about making sure that Calvin students knew where to go to vote, had transportation to the polls, and could effectively challenge any attempts to deny them the right to vote. On Election Day, they decorated the central quad with balloons, and held an on-campus parade urging everyone to cast their vote.

All of this was good work, similar to what many other DM chapters were doing. Calvin Democracy Matters had made the election an important focus of attention on campus, and undoubtedly convinced more students to register and vote than otherwise would have been the case. However, as proud as Alan was of the chapter's work and as impressed as he was with Stacy's organizing ability, he was worried. So when he talked with Stacy after the election, he praised the chapter's accomplishments, but also criticized the continuing absence of organizing around money in politics. Stacy reacted defensively. She maintained that the chapter wanted to include the issue of money in politics, but with so much other information to communicate, they just could not fit it in. She also mentioned that several DM members had believed that pointing out the power of wealthy donors would only add to students' political cynicism and actually discourage them from voting. But with the election now over and the semester winding down, Stacy assured Alan that the chapter would make the switch for the Spring semester.

It never happened. Over the next month, as the chapter planned for the spring, Stacy argued for several different projects on money in politics. However, most Calvin DM members wanted to continue to find ways to increase student voting. Intense discussions among the DM members resulted in their deciding that a campaign to establish a polling station on campus would be the focus of their spring organizing. Even after attending the DM Summit in early February, where Calvin DMers participated in discussions about money in politics, that issue still did not become a priority for the chapter. They organized an April film festival during DM's annual Week of Action. The four documentaries they presented were concerned with the safety of the food supply, the health care system, climate change, and economic inequality. Their intention was to orchestrate discussions following the films. At that time,they would point out the role campaign financing played in creating the problems the films revealed.

But Stacey had trouble finding chapter members other than herself willing to facilitate the post-film discussions. In the end hardly anyone—not even most chapter members—stayed to talk. In her May end-of-semester report, Stacy summed up the year's experience: "The main thing that I struggled with especially second semester was getting students energized about the issue of public campaign financing. When we were doing the stuff in the Fall we had great attendance. But it seemed that our most committed members were the least enthusiastic about working on money in politics. The more I pushed, the less that other students stepped up to do anything. We lost members to other groups. People felt there was nothing they could really do about campaign financing."

In May, Joan approached Stacy about working with DM for

another year. She hated to lose such an effective organizer. But she was not satisfied with what the Calvin DM chapter had done. We did not want DM's mission limited to increasing student voting rates. Joan made it clear that if we were to renew Stacy's internship, this time there would have to be an emphasis on money in politics from the start. Stacy replied that though she had really enjoyed being a campus coordinator and had learned a lot about politics, she could not commit to another year. She felt that the issue of money in politics was too "confrontational" to attract enough students at Calvin. But she added that personally she had found she really "liked politics," and was even thinking about running for office someday—"hopefully with public financing."

Over the years, we have had similar experiences on other campuses, where Democracy Matters did interesting and even valuable organizing, but struggled to put money and politics at the center of its work. As we did at Calvin, we made a concerted effort to work with such chapters and their interns to ensure that they advanced public campaign funding as the answer to the political dominance of wealth. On some campuses DMers made the switch. But unless chapters successfully did so, we did not renew their DM internship.

CHAPTER 8

BUILDING A SOCIAL MOVEMENT

Democracy Matters has now engaged in a thirteen-year on-campus experiment. The issue under investigation is whether students can be organized in support of the public funding of electoral campaigns. Our answer is yes.

During these years Democracy Matters has awarded internships to an average of fifty campus coordinators annually, though there have been variations in that number over time. We estimate that about 80 percent of these interns were successful at building Democracy Matters chapters on their campuses. Throughout the academic year, DM clubs were typically composed of ten to twelve core members. They educated and involved hundreds of students, faculty, and administrators. During this period under the auspices of Democracy Matters, roughly 400 interns organized campus political work. A multiple of that number—perhaps as many as 5,000 students—were core members of DM chapters. A much larger, but impossible-to-estimate, number of students and others actively participated in Democracy Matters activities.

All of this testifies to Democracy Matters' success. We have been able to teach eager students about the theory and practice of egalitarian democracy, as well as the principles of inclusion and respectful dialogue that should shape efforts at reform. We have also provided many young people with the practical tools necessary for effective political organizing. DM has become a substantial presence on campuses all over the country, as well as an acknowledged part of the national campaign finance reform community.

We have, however, remained a boutique organization. We have not scaled up to our potential. Even during our peak years—with upward of seventy campus chapters—DM was active at only a small percentage of the country's universities and colleges. Our constrained budget has meant we have not been able to test our limits. We really do not know how many interns we could recruit if we had more financing. Because of that, the typical American college student remains unexposed to both the urgency and the possibility of challenging the power of wealth in our political system. They do not know such efforts exist, and they have never heard of Democracy Matters.

It is possible that we have been lulled into an overly optimistic assessment of the potential of money in politics to act as a focal point for movement-building among students. Because it has been relatively easy for us to recruit interns, and because they have generally been successful in their campus organizing, it is conceivable that we have exaggerated the extent to which ours is a potentially popular and attractive issue on campuses.

While a certain amount of skepticism about our growth potential therefore might be appropriate, we very much doubt that we have reached anything like our maximum size. Since 2010, judicial decisions have unleashed a torrent of unregulated private money into the political process. If the distortions and biases associated with the use of wealth in politics were not clear in the past, they are now unambiguously obvious to all who pay even casual attention to current affairs. Because of that, it is all but certain that we would be able to greatly increase the number of DM interns if we had the resources with which to expand. We think that the public financing of election campaigns is a goal capable of attracting and energizing enough students to become an important component of a social movement to deepen democracy.

POTENTIAL

That such a movement does not exist is obvious. As we have discussed, inadequate funding is a problem in this regard. As a result, very few people in the United States are even aware that public financing is an alternative to the current private system of paying for electoral campaigns. This certainly is what we find to be the case on campuses. Over and over again, our experience has been that it comes as a revelation when we argue that electoral campaigns should be treated as a public good and that the option of public funding should be available to candidates for office.[33] There are of course people who in principle oppose using taxpayer money in this way. But that reaction is not typical. Rather, what we hear most often are expressions of interest, followed by a series of questions concerning how such a system would work in practice.

This lack of awareness on campus is replicated in the wider society. That public funding of electoral campaigns is not part of the political dialogue does not result from people's considering and rejecting it. It is a marginal issue and will remain so unless and until a social movement emerges that places it on the country's political agenda.

If such a movement were to appear, it would have to be initiated by progressives who believe that America should democratize its politics. At the moment there are few such individuals who see democratization as their priority political concern. Most progressives have deep attachments to specific policy outcomes. The list is long. The environment, same sex marriage, LGBTQ rights, educational reform, health care, gun control, poverty, food safety, animal rights, women's empowerment, labor law reform, and civil rights all have their adherents. Many of those involved in these projects are, or at least would be, sympathetic to legislation that would make public funds available to candidates. But they are almost always reluctant to commit strongly to the issue, though many would concede that the power of private contributions has seriously damaged their own causes. Typically for such individuals, campaign finance simply does not make the cut in the allocation of their time and energy.

Lying behind this reluctance is the reality that it is not possible to ensure specific policy outcomes even if the public funding of election campaigns were adopted. Changing the way politics is paid for is a process issue. It is true that such a reform will result in a deeper and more inclusive democracy. With increased political equality, a wider range of citizens will become effective participants in the country's politics than at present. But the fact remains that the actual policies and programs that will emerge from a more democratic process are necessarily uncertain. In a political system not dominated by private funding, the arguments that are most persuasive to a majority of citizens—not campaign contributions—will determine which policies are adopted. But there is no way in advance to accurately predict those outcomes.

However, there is a positive side to this indeterminacy. Because of its likely impact on multiple issues, the effort to achieve such a reform has the potential to attract a large percentage of progressive political activists. Public financing of campaigns might not be their top priority, but many could become convinced that the probability of success in their specific issue area will be significantly advanced with that reform. In addition, for these reformers as well as the general population, public financing could be attractive because of its promise to create a more egalitarian democratic process. The fact that public campaign financing is relevant to virtually everyone, but is a burning priority only to relatively few, captures both our difficulty and our opportunity.

The upshot is that the potential exists for public campaign financing to become the basis for building a broad and inclusive social movement. In most coalitions, members are asked to trade off some of their individual concerns in order to work with others in the name of a shared objective. But this is less the case for groups and individuals that might coalesce around reforming campaign financing. None of the participants would have to forgo their specific policy concerns. On the contrary, for them, activism on behalf of public financing would be a win-win situation. Its implementation would not only mean that their substantive policy issues would have an increased chance to prevail. In addition, they would be participants in an enriched democracy where money is less the arbiter of political power.

Ironically, that an effective coalition is possible to construct has been demonstrated by the political Right, and specifically by the power exercised by the Tea Party in the Republican Party. A recent study by Theda Skocpol and Vanessa Williamson argues that three determinants were critical to that success. The first is "grassroots activism," described by the authors as "a key force, energized by angry, conservative-minded citizens who have formed vital local and regional groups." The second is the "panoply of national funders and ultra-free-market advocacy groups that seek to highlight and leverage the grassroots efforts to further their long-term goal of remaking the Republican Party." The third and final source of the movement's strength is the media, in particular "conservative media hosts who openly espouse and encourage the cause." In sum, Skocpol and Williamson argue that each of these three "is important in its own right and their interaction is what gives the Tea Party its dynamism, drama and wallop. Grassroots activists, roving billionaire advocates and right-wing media purveyors—these three forces together create the Tea Party and give it the ongoing clout to buffet and redirect the Republican Party and influence broader debates in American democracy."[34]

On each of these three variables progressives, advocates of public financing, are especially at a distinct disadvantage compared to those to who created the Tea Party. With regard to the first variable cited by Skocpol and Williamson, right-wing grassroots activism is much more extensive than it is on the Left. Concerning the second, we do not possess nearly as many millionaires and billionaires ready to lavishly underwrite their political views. And lastly, at least in part because of the other two, the media generally enable conservatives to set the terms of political discussion. But those disadvantages, important as they may be, are not so great as to be fatal, rendering prospects for a movement for electoral democracy moot.

Media exposure is the least problematic of the three. It is certainly true that progressives have not been able to match the reach of right-wing radio talk-show hosts—the Glenn Becks and Rush Limbaughs of the world. But the fact is once Occupy Wall Street emerged in 2011, MSNBC as well as many mainstream newspapers and other media outlets provided extensive and often favorable coverage. Furthermore, on the subject of campaign finance reform, MSNBC offers a steady diet of left-of-center commentators—all of whom are hostile to the dominant role of wealth in politics and the torrent of private political money unleashed by Citizens United and other court decisions. Regular media reports on the amount, the sources, and the role of campaign money, especially during the run-up to elections, are ubiquitous. Some of these even embrace the need for reform. For example, in February 2012, the editorial page of the *New York Times* explicitly endorsed public campaign financing. It called for a statewide public funding option to address what it referred to as the "corrupting mess" of money in politics and the "scandalously lax campaign finance laws" in New York State.[35]

The media, then, is not our principle problem. But the fact that progressives have largely given up on grassroots organizing is. Efforts in recent years by those on the political Left to bring large numbers of people together—on the ground and in the streets—have been few and far between. The migration to the Washington Beltway undertaken in the past by liberal advocacy organizations was a choice, not a necessity. It certainly was not something that the emergence of new technologies of communication dictated. Indeed, our experience over

a lifetime of political engagement makes it perfectly clear that inno-
vations like the Internet, email, and social media have made it easier
and more feasible to do movement-building than in the past. The
Democracy Matters staff today provides information to DM activists
in real time, material that would have arrived only much later if, as
in the past, we were limited to using the postal service. Similarly the
Internet as a research tool means that we now easily have access to
and distribute far larger volumes of information on both organizing
and money in politics than we ever could have in the past.

Social media, too, can facilitate organizing. Skocpol and
Williamson illustrate this nicely in their discussion of the emergence
of the Tea Party. They report that when a retired individual and a few
of his acquaintances in Virginia decided to form a group, his experience with social media became crucial to their efforts. Previously he
had used a "meet-up" site to assemble a volunteer group to fight
Attention Deficit Disorder. To his friends in what would later become
the Tea Party, he explained that meet-up can "help you get organized
in a hurry." And it worked. "Before long, dozens of . . . Peninsula
Patriots were gathering monthly to hear speakers and plan for rallies,
lobbying, and local advocacy."[36]

The new technology represents an important tool for social movements. But it is no substitute for grassroots organizing. Building a
strong movement requires the rallies, the local groups, and the network of face-to-face relationships that only grassroots organizing can
effectively construct. The problem with DC-based advocacy organizations is that they rely too much on electronic communication.
When those groups talk about a field operation, it is more likely
to involve E-alerts and E-newsletters than it is to put experienced

organizers in the field to bring together local and regional groups.

The bulk of the responsibility for the absence of a progressive social movement rests on funders, particularly the big liberal foundations. Financing is critical to any activity. As we have detailed, funders tend to shy away from controversial projects, lack a long-term time horizon, and are therefore not interested in grassroots organizing that possesses an explicitly political objective. To the extent that foundations deny the resources activists require, they bear the principle responsibility for the absence of a mobilized population on the Left.

It is plausible to argue that the absence of funding for grassroots organizing results from foundations receiving few such requests. Problems are thereby created on the demand side by organizations seeking funding, as well as on the supply side by foundations offering grants. Both of these factors are at work and are mutually reinforcing. But the main burden does fall on the funders. Progressive organizations know that foundations have a record of denying grants to political organizing projects. Thus they rationally refrain from requesting such funds. No funder ever claimed that Democracy Matters was denied funding because we were doing a poor job of student organizing. Rather, they simply did not want to pay for what we thought was important.

Of course, not all progressives confine themselves to an insider strategy. Occupy Wall Street did exactly the opposite. It brought people into the streets. But it inflicted marginalization on itself by refusing to engage the political system. Notwithstanding this weakness, Occupy allowed the widespread dissatisfaction with growing inequality that is present in the country to surface. That discontent was intense enough to bring large numbers of people militantly into the streets. But because Occupy failed to provide any outlet aside from street occupations, the insurgency faded. Its organizers ignored the fact that taking to the streets cannot be an end in itself. There has to be a second level of electoral and legislative activity, and associated with that second level there have to be victories. People will not indefinitely engage in projects that fail to show results. In short, having committed itself to an apolitical one-dimensional stance, Occupy's shelf-life was short.

Tea Party activists made no such mistake. They had their rallies and their street demonstrations. But they were single-minded with regard to the vehicle by which they sought to achieve their objectives. Their intention was to reshape the Republican Party in their own image. The mechanisms for doing so were primary elections. Republican candidates for office knew that organized Tea Party activists were prepared to challenge them in primary races if they fell short of meeting stringent political and policy tests—foremost of which was the miniaturization of government. The threat was a real one, and more than one incumbent fell to a Tea Party electoral insurgency. In the process, the entire Republican establishment responded by moving sharply to the right.

Right-wing insurgents articulated an easily understood and concrete political goal behind which large numbers of people, no matter their other disagreements, could rally. Reducing the size of government was their mantra, and the means to do so was all but universally attractive: reduce taxes. They did not have to specify which programs or projects would be cut—those decisions could be ducked. First priority was assigned to reducing government revenues. The resulting budget deficits would seem to make cutting public expenditures a necessity in the name of commonsense fiscal responsibility. This was the genius of Grover Norquist's litmus test that candidates pledge never to vote for a tax increase.

To date, progressives have lacked such a unifying strategy. We urgently need one. Social movements require a vision to inspire activist commitment and work. What is required is a policy objective with which a large swath of left-of-center individuals agree and which at the same time advances the personal agenda of each of them.

Greater political equality achieved through public campaign financing is our candidate to fill that function. Our experiences on university campuses have taught us that a receptive audience exists for the argument that reducing the role of private wealth in politics is a decisive first step in achieving a more progressive United States. We can be convincing that the resulting enriched and deepened democracy could be the vehicle to construct a better America.

To do this we need political organizers who, even as they seek radically to reorganize the political system, are willing to participate in it. Their task will be to attract large numbers to the cause. As was the case on campus, we anticipate that most of those initial recruits will be people who are disgusted by the current "pay to play" system and seek a more just and equitable politics. There are many such individuals, and they will have to be mobilized as the pioneers of the movement.

But to reach a critical mass, the movement will have to extend beyond those already predisposed to campaign finance reform. We will have to work to attract activists who work on other projects. Among others, these could include the considerable numbers of individuals already part of organizations actively pursuing progressive objectives. Environmentalists who have seen the threat of global climate change ignored, union members who have seen management successfully win legislation that eviscerates organized labor, and people of color and women whose difficulty in raising campaign funds results in their being significantly underrepresented in elective office—all these might join such a movement. In addition, middle- and low-income people who have been the principle victims of inadequacies and cutbacks in public spending, and others worried that growing cynicism and political apathy are undermining the country's democracy—they too might be convinced to speak out against the dominating political power of wealth.

In this movement as in many of the past, students will need to play a special role. Historically, young people have provided a moral compass for their elders, highlighting the need for social change. They have also been an important source of energy and innovative thinking. These will be required again. But because today's students share the population's political cynicism, motivating them to engage in activism will not be an easy task. It will require, as we have learned, face-to-face interaction, committed mentors, patience, and long-term involvement. The social liberalism possessed by many members of the current generation of young people and their knowledge that in the future they will have to live with society's unsolved problems may, under the right circumstances, be sufficient to encourage them to participate in a movement for democratic change and political equality.

The Occupy Wall Street mistake has to be avoided. The success of a new reform movement will be measured by whether it can pass legislation that effectively increases the influence of citizens by reducing donor power. Opposition will be fierce. The vast financial resources that wealthy special interests possess will be deployed in an effort to defeat reform. But the only way to democratize politics is by changing the laws. To be victorious, the political mobilization of many people will be required to trump the power of wealth.

Democracy Matters' experience has shown that young people, as in the past, can play an important role in a democratic renaissance. Their potential in that regard has barely been tapped. Indeed, it has been largely ignored by adult organizations. For that reason, the full expression of that latent capability awaits the time when the older generation—on campus and off—provides the support the younger generation requires. Money will be needed. But so too will be the participation of experienced activists who understand the power of grassroots movements and the importance of legislation in creating lasting radical change.

Our hope was (and is) that Democracy Matters on campus will help to create an active student movement—filling the role that students played during the Civil Rights era, when young people both triggered the conscience of the country and identified how, through legislation, greater political equality could be achieved. Democracy Matters has demonstrated the feasibility of such a movement.

ENDNOTES

[1] An American National Election Studies (ANES) survey in 2008, the last year for which data are available, reported that 63 percent of respondents disapproved of Congress's performance and that 69 percent believed that the government is run for the benefit of a few big interests. *ANES Guide to Public Opinion and Electoral Behavior*, http://electionstudies.org/nesguide/. See Tables 5C.4 and 5A.2.

[2] Larry M. Bartels, *Unequal Democracy: The Political Economy of the New Gilded Age* (Princeton/Oxford: Princeton University Press, 2008), 257-60.

[3] In 2010, for example, the Center reported that what it refers to as a "tiny elite," 0.12 percent of the population, donated a total of $773, 463,104 to federal campaigns. See http://www.opensecrets.org/overview/donordemographics.php.

[4] Center for Responsive Politics, "Stats at a Glance," and "Outside Spending," http://www. opensecrets.org.

[5] For more on treating elections as a public good see, Jay R. Mandle, *Creating Political Equality: American Elections as a Public Good* (Palo Alto, CA: Academica Press, 2010), 1–15.

[6] Systems of full public financing were implemented in states including Maine and Arizona as early as 1996. In Maine, the Clean

Elections Act was passed as the result of a citizen initiative, winning 55 percent of the vote, and taking 15 out of 16 counties in the state. For more information, see https://www5.informe.org/online/ethics/cleanelection/faq/.

[7] Maine Citizens for Clean Elections, "2002–2010 General Election Comparison," http://www.mainecleanelections.org/assets/files/ce2010generalanalysis2011.pdf.

[8] In a 2008 ANES survey asking whether the government should provide fewer services such as education and health, on a scale ranging from one to seven where one was "cut services/spending" and seven was "more services/spending," 24 percent of respondents ranked themselves as one to three and 41 percent placed themselves as five to seven. *ANES Guide to Public Opinion and Electoral Behavior*, Table 4A.5.

[9] According to Herbert E. Alexander, the Nixon campaign spent $62 million, while the McGovern campaign spent $30 million. Herbert E. Alexander, *Financing the 1972 Election* (Lexington, MA: Lexington Books, 1976), Table 4.4 and Table 4.5, 85–86.

[10] Julian E. Zelizer, "Seeds of Cynicism: The Struggle Over Campaign Finance, 1956–1974," in Paula Baker (ed.), *Money and Politics*, (University Park: Pennsylvania State University Press, 2002), 83, 74.

[11] R. Sam Garrett, "The State of Campaign Finance Policy: Recent Development and Issues for Congress" (Washington, DC: Congressional Research Service, April 29, 2011), 8.

[12] Gabriela Schneider, "Editorial Memo: This Election Proves We Need Campaign Finance Transparency Now," The Sunlight Foundation, November 8, 2012, http://sunlightfoundation.com.

[13] John H. Pryor, Linda DeAngelo, Laura Palucki Blake, Sylvia Hurtado, and Serge Tran, *The American Freshman: National Norms*

Fall 2011 (Berkeley, Los Angeles, London: University of California Press, 2011) 39, 40. In the survey 21.7 percent chose "conservative" and 1.8 percent selected "far right."

[14] Ibid., 31.

[15] To protect students' privacy, we will be using only their first names throughout the book.

[16] David Graeber, "Occupy Wall Street's Anarchist Roots," in Janet Byrne (ed.) *The Occupy Handbook,* (New York, Boston, London: Back Bay Books, 2012), 144. See also New York City General Assembly, "Principles of Solidarity," http://www.nycga.net/resources/principle-of-solidarity; and New York City General Assembly, "Declaration of the Occupation of New York," http://www.nycga.net/resources/declaration.

[17] Theda Skocpol, *Diminished Democracy: From Membership to Management in American Civic Life* (Norman: University of Oklahoma Press, 2003), 138, 135.

[18] Ibid., 138, 141, 144.

[19] This paragraph and the next are based on J. Craig Jenkins, "Channeling Social Protest: Foundation Patronage of Contemporary Social Movements," in W. W. Powell and Elisabeth S. Clemens (eds.), *Private Action and the Public Good,* (New Haven/London: Yale University Press, 1998), 207–14.

[20] The exception to this pattern was the Rockefeller Brothers Fund, which has continued to provide us with small grants over a number of years. The program officer at that foundation was himself previously a teacher and perhaps better understood more than others the importance of intensive education and organizing with young people.

[21] For a discussion of the small donor strategy see Jay R. Mandle, *Creating Political Equality: American Elections as a Public Good,* 49–65.

[22] Andrew McFarland, *Common Cause: Lobbying in the Public Interest* (Chatham, NJ: Chatham House, 1984), 26, 106.

[23] John Dalton and Pamela Crosby, "From Volunteering to Voting: Higher Education's Role in Preparing College Students for Political Engagement," *Journal of College & Character,* 9/4 (April 2008) 1.

[24] American Association of State Colleges and Universities, "The Leadership Association of Public Colleges and Universities Delivering America's Promise: About ADP," http://www.aascu.org/programs/adp/.

[25] Association of American Colleges and Universities, "Strategic Plan 2008-2012: Aim High and Make Excellence Inclusive," http://www.aacu.org/About/Strategic_Plan.cfm.

[26] See http://campuscompact.org.

[27] Civic Learning and Education Project, "About the CLDE Project," http://www.civiclearning.org; U.S. Department of Education, "US Department of Education Calls for Action to Develop 21st Century Citizens, Strengthen Democracy," January 10, 2012, http://www.ed.gov/news/press-releases/.

[28] See http://www.compact.org/program-models/program-models-campus-wide-service-events/greek-can-serve-a-thon/2124/.

[29] Anne Colby, Elizabeth Beaumont, Thomas Ehrlich, and Josh Corngold, *Educating for Democracy: Preparing Undergraduates for Responsible Political Engagement* (San Francisco: Jossey-Bass, 2007), 4, 41.

[30] Jon Dalton and Pamela Crosby, "From Volunteering to Voting: Higher Education's Role in Preparing College Students for Political Engagement," *Journal of College & Character* 9/4 (April 2008), 2.

[31] Elizabeth Hollander and Nicholas V. Longo, "Student Political Engagement and the Renewal of Democracy," *Journal of College and Character* 10/1 (September 2008). See also K. Edward Spiezi, "Pedagogy and Political (Dis)Engagement," *Liberal Education* (Fall 2002), available at http://aacu.org/liberaleducation/le-fa02/le-fa02feature2.cfm.

[32] Kerry Strand, "Democracy Matters on Campus," *Footnotes*, American Sociological Association (November 2001), http://www.asanet.org/footnotes/nov01/fn5/html.

[33] Jay R. Mandle, "The Political Market," *Journal of Economic Issues* 47/1, March, 2013, 135–46.

[34] Theda Skocpol and Venessa Williamson, *The Tea Party and the Remaking of Republican Conservatism* (New York: Oxford University Press, 2012), 12–13.

[35] Editorial, "While We Wait for Reform," *New York Times*, February 15, 2012, http://www.nytimes.com/2012/02/16/opinion/new-york-waits-for-campaign-finance-reform.html?r=2&scp=2&sq=cuomopercent20public percent20financing&st=cse.

[36] Theda Skocpol and Venessa Williamson, *The Tea Party and the Remaking of Republican Conservatism*, 85.

ABOUT THE AUTHORS

Joan D. Mandle, Ph.D., has been Executive Director of Democracy Matters since 2001. She was the Director of Women's Studies and Associate Professor of Sociology and Anthropology at Colgate University from 1990-2001. Her political activism as well as her research, teaching, and publications center on social movements and social change in America. She is the recipient of the "Lifetime Feminist Activism" award from the Sociologists for Women in Society.

Jay R. Mandle, Ph.D., is the W. Bradford Wiley Professor of Economics at Colgate University. He specialies in and has written widely on poverty, economic globalization, and the process of economic development in the United States and abroad. He publishes as well on the economics of democracy. A life-long activist, he was one of the founders of Democracy Matters, with the goal of creating a more equal and fair political system.

Adonal Foyle is a retired NBA player, who was the eighth overall NBA draft pick in 1997. He played a total of 13 NBA seasons, first with the Golden State Warriors and then with the Orlando Magic and Memphis Grizzlies. He later served as the Director of Player Development with Orlando. He is a founder and the president of Democracy Matters. Adonal also created the Kerosene Lamp Foundation (www.KLFkids.org), that uses basketball to engage and empower at-risk youth in the Caribbean and USA.

Democracy Matters organizes college students to fight against the takeover of our elections and our democracy by wealthy campaign contributors. With grassroots organizing on college campuses, Democracy Matters encourages and facilitates non-partisan student political activism.

To learn more, visit www.democracymatters.org.